The Magnitude of Us

Advance Praise for *The Magnitude of Us*

"Unlearning the HUSH means moving, through pedagogy and instructional planning, toward the deepest elements of education: compassion, self reflection, perspective taking, critical analysis. It means challenging assumptions and positionalities. And it means believing in the power of story to make a difference, to sew the first patch in a quilt of awakened understanding."

—**Brittany Collins**, educator and author of *Learning From Loss*

"*The Magnitude of Us* is a masterful text that brings to light once-marginalized stories of the past to inspire our work in classrooms. Magisterially written and replete with resources and inspiring histories, Dr. Marlee Bunch weaves a rich tapestry of struggle, celebration, and inspiration that few scholars can achieve in a book that promises to improve our praxis."

—**Jon Hale**, associate professor of education policy, organization, and leadership, University of Illinois Urbana–Champaign

"Dr. Bunch's framework and guide provides important and critical ways for educators and students to delve into processes of unlearning the silences of those who have been historically marginalized. This is an important step toward corrective action for culturally responsive and sustaining pedagogies, and applicable across the K–12 spectrum."

—**Yoon Pak**, professor and head of education policy, organization, and leadership, University of Illinois Urbana–Champaign

"Dr. Bunch's un/HUSH framework is a wellspring of inspiration for educators. Her research, pedagogical framework, and reflection questions are powerful tools to help inservice and preservice teachers examine their positionality and apply an equity lens to their lesson planning. Lessons from the past guide the way to create empowering learning environments for students in K–12 and higher education. Activities centering storytelling and healing motivate and sustain educators in the critical work of maximizing cultural responsiveness in their classrooms and communities."

—**Carol Berner**, lecturer, Department of Education and Child Study, Smith College

"Marlee is brilliant and so is this book."

—**Ava Dellaira**, author of *Love Letters to the Dead*

The Magnitude of Us

An Educator's Guide to Creating Culturally Responsive Classrooms

Marlee S. Bunch

Foreword by Joyce A. Ladner

Afterword by Brittany R. Collins

TEACHERS COLLEGE PRESS
TEACHERS COLLEGE | COLUMBIA UNIVERSITY
NEW YORK AND LONDON

Published by Teachers College Press,® 1234 Amsterdam Avenue, New York, NY 10027

Front cover painting by Mario Joyce. Background texture by Mick Haupt / Unsplash.

Library of Congress Cataloging-in-Publication Data

Names: Bunch, Marlee S., author. | Ladner, Joyce A., author of foreword. | Collins, Brittany R., author of afterword.
Title: The magnitude of us : an educator's guide to creating culturally responsive classrooms / Marlee S. Bunch ; foreword by Joyce Ladner ; afterword by Brittany R. Collins.
Description: New York, NY : Teachers College Press, [2024] | Includes bibliographical references and index. | Summary: "A blueprint for utilizing histories, culturally responsive teaching, and community responsive pedagogy to build collaborative and equitable classrooms (7th grade-College) Includes scaffolding and lesson plans"— Provided by publisher.
Identifiers: LCCN 2024012314 (print) | LCCN 2024012315 (ebook) | ISBN 9780807769881 (paper ; acid-free paper) | ISBN 9780807769898 (hardcover; acid-free paper) | ISBN 9780807782484 (ebook)
Subjects: LCSH: Culturally relevant pedagogy—United States. | Critical pedagogy—United States. | History—Methodology. | Multicultural education—United States. | Educational equalization—United States. | Community and school—United States. | Community and college—United States. | Group work in education—United States. | Teaching—Social aspects—United States.
Classification: LCC LC1099.515.C85 B86 2024 (print) | LCC LC1099.515.C85 (ebook) | DDC 370.11/5—c23/eng/20240615
LC record available at https://lccn.loc.gov/2024012314
LC ebook record available at https://lccn.loc.gov/2024012315

ISBN 978-0-8077-6988-1 (paper)
ISBN 978-0-8077-6989-8 (hardcover)
ISBN 978-0-8077-8248-4 (ebook)

Printed on acid-free paper
Manufactured in the United States of America

We are each other's
harvest:
we are each other's
business:
we are each other's
magnitude and bond.

—Gwendolyn Brooks

This book is dedicated to the ancestors and educators who paved a path forward and created possibilities during impossible times. Let us always remember their lessons and be inspired by their ability to hope and dream and love.

This book is dedicated to my amazing former students: Elijah, Miyah, Xyanne, Munira, Imani, Michaela, Will, Tyree, Alexis, Katie, Cassidy, Cierra, Mayra, Keeshon, Domonique, Marcus, Zoie, Myles, Alisha, Charlotte, Gage, Jazz, Rochelle, and the many *others I have had the honor of teaching and mentoring throughout the years. I am the educator and advocate I am because of what I learned from you. The years we spent together learning and growing were some of the best times of my life. I am so proud of you. I love and appreciate you and am honored that you are my legacy.*

This book is also dedicated to any student or educator who has ever felt unseen or unheard—you are valued and important.

To Chrissy and all preservice and new educators—this is for you.

Contents

Foreword

Dr. Marlee Bunch's research and teaching framework leads me to recall my own experiences growing up and reflect on how those experiences connect to the now. *The Magnitude of Us* and the un/HUSH teaching framework speak to the fact that the past can inform classroom activities and move us toward equitable spaces. Dr. Bunch is breaking new ground as she shows how the intersections of past and present are, in and of themselves, a resource for educators.

Unlike scores of American women who were taught to hush, hush up, and make themselves invisible, Black women in America during my era were never taught that at home. I was never taught that. We were given enormous responsibilities throughout our lives, starting when we were kids. In the South, we often came from large families, which required the older kids to look after their younger siblings. We all had jobs and expectations; we were our mother's helper. We did not have the luxury of living with carefree abandon. Womanhood came early to us, and childhood was a distant invention not often afforded to us. The issues we faced in my time are not too different from our concerns today. We knew our larger responsibilities, both at home and civically. The methods used by Black teachers inculcated the strengths and the tried-and-true formulas for student and personal success, instead of focusing on weaknesses and failures. They modeled the best of Black culture for their students, which, in turn, gave students a positive identity and a "can do" spirit.

Research tells us that the majority of teachers now are white females. Black women exited teaching when schools in the South began to desegregate, causing massive displacement of Black teachers. I recall reading about a Black principal who had been reassigned to work as a janitor. So much history, values, and culture were destroyed and abandoned. Children not only were placed in new environments (white environments) as second-class citizens but also lost what helped solidify their emerging identities. They lost their advocates and the teachers who believed in them and inspired them to learn. They lost teachers who believed there was no such thing as an ineducable child, teachers who would make home visits if they missed too many days of school. They lost teachers as role models in their communities—the teachers who loved and respected them. Our Black teachers invested tremendously in us because they saw us as their replacements. They wanted us to go forth and carry out the goals they were attempting to carry out and accomplish in society.

Now, there is an obliteration of Black history and marginalized histories. It has been a couple of generations since Black teachers played this critical role in the lives of Black students. I believe that many of the barriers for Black children to achieve are related to this disconnect between themselves and teachers who embrace them fully. They no longer have teachers who look like them, who go the extra mile, who instill self-confidence and self-identity. Black and Brown children need role models who truly believe in their ability to achieve.

We need to return to a time that lifts up students through the history, storytelling, and narratives that were provided by these teachers from a bygone era, putting them at the center of classroom activities and learning experiences for students. If we can recapture the sentiments, the expertise, the values, and the teaching styles of past Black educators, we can work toward reform. We can work toward helping all students feel valued.

If all these things were to become a part of teacher education, and if new and existing teachers were asked to enter and re-enter their classrooms with this renewed set of methods guided by the voices of women who were never hushed, then going forward, I predict we would have far better educational outcomes. The framework and guidebook offered in *The Magnitude of Us* can help all educators work to do just this. History, stories, unlearning, and healing are all aspects that work not only toward empowering children and sustaining them to learn unimpeded, like generations before them, but also to give them encouragement to be deeply involved in their own education and learning.

—Dr. Joyce A. Ladner
Civil Rights Activist, Educator, Sociologist, and Author

Acknowledgments

This book and framework were inspired by the oral histories of educators and students who navigated integration and schooling in Mississippi between 1954 and 1971. Thank you for your oral histories and for your contributions to education. To Mrs. Armstrong, Mrs. Heath, Mrs. Goins, Mrs. Woullard, Mrs. Hale-Green, Mrs. Fowler, Mrs. Bobbitt, Mrs. Manning, Mrs. Ellie Dahmer, Ms. Bettie Dahmer, Dr. Ladner, Mrs. Smith, Mrs. Jones, Mr. Cooper, and Secretary Lonnie Bunch: I am humbled to have heard your stories and shared time with you. You are all such heroes—my heroes. I will never forget your contributions, lessons, lived truths, and memories. Knowing I walk in your greatness is an empowering and beautiful history. Thank you for your vision, strength, and love. Thank you to *all* educators who strive to be excellent, challenge the system, enrich the lives of students, and who ultimately are the bedrock of this world.

Dr. Span—Thank you for being my mentor, for inspiring me, and for being kin. This book would not have been possible without you. You have always believed in me, which is the most empowering gift. Thank you for modeling what true leadership and mentorship embody.

Dr. Lee—Thank you for your guidance and encouragement. I am so grateful.

Dr. Hale, Dr. Pak, and Dr. Wyatt—Thank you for your generous support.

Mr. Charles Cooper—Thank you for wisdom and for being extended family.

Dr. Ladner—Thank you for being my GodMomma. You are a foot soldier extraordinaire.

Thank you to the the University of Illinois and the TEAACH team, Dr. Griswold at Cal State, Carol at Smith College, Michelle at PEBC, Lisa at Baltimore County Schools, Pam and Dimitry at Facing History, the Dee Dee Jackson Foundation, Good Black Art, and Race Project KC for giving me a space to grow and explore the un/HUSH framework and myself. I am ever grateful.

Sarah and Teachers College Press—Thank you for everything. Sarah, thank you for truly understanding the importance of this project, for making this journey wonderful, and for your incredible support. Working with you has been such a gift.

The artists who contributed gifts of poetry, words, time, and art—Thank you to Jordan Stempleman, Emily Pettit, Ashley Jones, Claudia Rankine, Evie Shockley, Cole Swensen, Mary Ruefle, Stanley Banks, Glenn North, Natasha Ria El-Scari, Kevin Hopkins, Brittany Collins (Frack), Gholdy Muhammad, Victoria Stempleman, and many others. Your artistry is so important and deeply valued. Mario Joyce—I feel endless gratitude for you sharing your artwork to grace the cover. Your work is inspiring and moving and such an important contribution to the world.

The many who collaborated—Thank you for sharing time and expertise, creating, inspiring, and making this a collaborative endeavor filled with an abundance of love.

Kennedy, Shana, Elon, Christy, Nathan, Cari, and many other loved ones—thank you for broadening my world and all of your support.

Amber—I am ever grateful that the start of our teaching journey led us to find each other.

Carrie—Thank you for being the person who brought days of sunshine in high school and the years after.

My friends and family—You are everything. Momma and Grandmom—Thank you for loving me whole, for filling my world with love, and for believing that I can do anything. Damian, Bella, Townes, Aiden, Bella B., Jordan, V, and Momma—You are the most important people in my life—words are not enough. I love you. Always.

The Magnitude of Us

Introduction

> won't you celebrate with me
> what i have shaped into
> a kind of life?
>
> —Lucille Clifton

As a young girl, I did not have dreams of being a teacher. In fact, I had no idea what I would do. I thought maybe I would be a singer, a writer, or a psychologist. Teaching, however, never crossed my mind until college, when I decided that I wanted to provide students with what I had missed out on in my own K–12 experiences. I had learned through my own education what *not* to do.

My K–12 education was far from equitable. I spent the first two years of elementary school in the neighborhood public school, and then the remainder in private schools. Growing up poor and in a less than desirable neighborhood in Kansas City meant I would have to either attend the local public school that was deemed failing or attend a private school. My grandmother made the decision to send me to a private school with the hope that it would provide me with a "good" education.

For all intents and purposes, I was a student who was likely deemed a "high risk student." Like many people, I had experienced a substantial number of challenges that did not make me appear to be college bound.

Attending a private school, there was no hiding how poor I was. This school was predominantly wealthy and white, and it was clear that I did not fit in. Out of my element and struggling socially, my grades by the end of 9th grade plummeted from straight As; by sophomore year, I had lost the academic scholarship that had given my grandmother financial relief from the crippling tuition. My high school years caused my innate love of learning to temporarily diminish as I grappled with how to navigate the social challenges that I faced in an environment that was unwelcoming.

I did not see myself anywhere in the schools I attended—not in the books, the teachers, or the curriculum. Representation in classrooms and in curriculum matters has the potential to deeply affect students. The lack of culturally responsive teaching practices (which connect students' cultures and lived experiences to curriculum and academic content) in my classrooms as a child and as an adolescent left an impact on me.

Thankfully, college would revive my love of learning. It opened a new world of literature, compelling courses, discussions, professors I connected with, and spaces that valued varied perspectives. It allowed me an opportunity to experience what a safe learning space felt like and, because of this, it cemented a lifelong love of learning. I loved it, and I thrived. College mirrored to me the best version of myself, and in those moments, I realized that there was nothing more powerful than an education involving equity, representation, and invested teachers.

In college, I would begin collecting what I found most impactful to bring to my future classroom. I would curate the things I appreciated most: the discussions, the exposure to a wide array of texts, the mentorship, and the collaboration. I would become a teacher who would find ways to create spaces and lessons where students could find and see elements of themselves.

My students have always been an inspiration, and much of my own personal growth has stemmed from the important interactions I have had in the classroom with them. We worked collaboratively to learn from and with one another. We centered stories and respect, and together those elements allowed transformations to occur. Those moments led me to be here with you, in the hopes that something from my teaching journey and research might help you build and sustain classrooms that listen to the voices of students, celebrate their uniqueness, and create spaces that foster authentic, culturally responsive, and meaningful learning.

CULTURALLY AND COMMUNITY IMMERSIVE PEDAGOGY

This teaching guidebook will help educators navigate emerging best practices to center historically marginalized voices and perspectives in middle, secondary, and postsecondary learning spaces.

It also provides an accessible framework for utilizing histories, culturally responsive teaching, and community responsive pedagogy to build collaborative and equitable classrooms. Inspired by research steeped in oral histories, it brings forth lessons from current and past educators, merged with the voices of students, to share impactful classroom practices.

One aspect that makes this book different from other resources on creating culturally responsive classrooms is that it extends the idea that culturally responsive teaching *alone* is not enough—we must be immersive. Culturally and community immersive pedagogy involves being culturally responsive and community responsive, moving our pedagogy into thinking that requires us to be immersed with others in conversation, in collaboration, and in community. (See Figure I.1.)

Invoking many of the teachings from the bell hooks (2003) text *Teaching Community*, community responsiveness requires immersion in communities and the act of being in community with others. Knowledge alone will not build cultural and historical awareness and responsiveness, but immersion embodies the core of such practices. Community immersive pedagogy acknowledges the nuances that we learn when we are in spaces with others; cultural responsiveness alone does not provide that information and can mislead educators into believing that if they know enough to be culturally competent, their work is complete. Being in community requires action, proximity, and immersion. Immersion is the action of being engaged, dedicated, collaborative, and involved. This way of thinking led me to not only develop the un/HUSH framework but also better understand my own practices and growth. Being immersed in practice with others—in community—is what allows us to expand our own perspectives and knowledge.

THE ORIGINS OF THIS BOOK

This book and the framework within it were born out of my doctoral research as well as my teaching experience. There are many tools and frameworks available to teachers, but what seems to be missing from the picture is the voices and experiences of past educators who could offer their guidance and expertise. Many of those teachers navigated times not too different from today. What can we learn from them? How can we use oral histories, lived experience,

Figure I.1. Collaboration and Being in Community

COLLABORATION AND BEING IN COMMUNITY

by Dr. Marlee Bunch and Brittany R. Collins

1: GOOD PARTNERSHIPS

Good partnerships can create the following benefits:

- Challenge and expand our thinking.
- Allow us to use our areas of expertise, while learning from someone else.
- Build community and relationships.
- Confront discomfort.
- Unearth half-formed thoughts.

2: CHARACTERISTICS

Characteristics of good collaboration include:

- Active listening.
- Ability to have fun.
- Vulnerability and honesty.
- Mutual respect.
- Shared purpose/goals.
- Aspects that challenge our thinking/growth.
- Open mindedness.
- Ability to safely disagree.

3: REFLECT AND CONSIDER

Who have you collaborated well with in the past? What energy do you bring to a collaboration? What type of energy do you need? What qualities do you contribute to a partnership? What do you most value in a collaborator? What lessons might you hope to learn? What might you hope to unlearn?

4. SELF-WORK

Collaboration asks us to unlearn and relearn. Self-work precedes the ability to effectively collaborate. Self-work may look like:

- Practicing freewriting or journaling.
- Processing and sharing challenging stories.
- Going to therapy.
- Sharing honest feedback with a peer.
- Identifying and advocating for your needs.
- Letting go of performativity or perfectionism.
- Understanding where your beliefs and emotional reactions come from.

5. HEALING

Self-work and collaboration involve healing. In partnership, this may look like:

- Naming and sharing honest emotions and reactions.
- Asking open-ended questions.
- Communicating needs and boundaries.
- Discussing your working relationship in addition to the work involved.
- Identifying and complementing each others' strengths and areas for growth.
- Sharing the work equitably.

"ONE OF THE MOST VITAL WAYS WE SUSTAIN OURSELVES IS BY BUILDING COMMUNITIES OF RESISTANCE, PLACES WHERE WE KNOW WE ARE NOT ALONE." -BELL HOOKS

and stories to forge relationships and engage collaboratively with one another?

Mentorship is powerful. We walk in the path of ancestry and mentors who made it possible for us to exist. The guidance and wisdom from the participants in my doctoral research (discussed below) instilled a sense of hope and possibility in me as an educator that was transformative. These educators' stories and inspiring efforts changed my life. I share their lessons and insights through this book and framework in hopes that they might offer you the same sense of empowerment and a renewed vision to sustain the important work we must do for future generations and students.

The Research

My research was a quest to understand the historical nature of some of the challenges educators face today and how these challenges are inevitably linked to the past (Zirkel, 2005). The purpose of my study was to examine the ways in which desegregation efforts and *Brown v. Board* impacted the lives of Black female educators from 1954 to 1971 in Hattiesburg, Mississippi. The study explored the lives and stories of these women, examined the historical implications of public school desegregation in Hattiesburg, and drew connections between history and current-day concerns in K–12 schools. This work helps extend our understanding of the oral histories of these Black women, fills gaps in the historical record, and centers the voices and histories of the Black women who forged the path for education in Mississippi.

My methodology for this research included oral history and historical research methods, using the oral histories of participants as primary sources. The study serves as a counterstory to the dominant narrative. Using counterstorytelling examines how these women's teaching experiences and oral histories push back on traditional narratives and constructs about race. Participants were Black women who taught pre- and post desegregation in Hattiesburg. My data collection occurred through Zoom and/or telephone interviews to collect and record the oral histories of my participants. Triangulation occurred using not only the oral histories of the Black female educators I interviewed, but also the oral histories of students who attended these schools, historians, and current-day educators. In documenting the oral histories and lived experiences of Black female educators, I came to understand their teaching philosophies, recommendations for creating classrooms and community, and the way in which they coupled activism and pedagogy to help their students better understand the world and themselves. Some of the messages that reverberated loudly included the importance of Black spaces, the use of creativity in the classroom, the role of history and storytelling, and how these aspects helped to create a sense of community, safety, healing, and inspiration—even in segregated Jim Crow Mississippi amidst racial violence and turmoil.

Deeply inspired by my research participants' stories and experiences, I wanted to create a resource that captured what I had learned from them. These lessons can be used to guide us in how to best approach education, classrooms, community, and mentorship, which will ultimately help us create culturally relevant spaces (Siddle Walker, 2000). The teaching that participants were committed to involved civic engagement, creativity, a whole-child teaching approach, and creating spaces that affirmed students. Once we unlearn the hushing of stories and silencing of voices and histories, we can move toward embracing the magnitude of what creates a community—us.

The un/HUSH Framework

The un/HUSH framework (Figure I.2) was developed based on the lessons I learned from my doctoral research and teaching experience and offers a guide that can be used in a classroom or learning space to employ many of the interpersonal and pedagogical approaches to teaching and learning that the participants of my research utilized. Through applying this lens and philosophy, we can ensure that we self-reflect *and* find actionable ways to create meaningful changes in the spaces where we teach and learn. These actions will ultimately help support the social, emotional, cultural, and academic development of teachers, students, and community members.

The framework is intended to help us avoid the "hush" by using its primary principles to guide our pedagogy. Using the acronym un/H-U-S-H serves as a visual reminder of what we are striving to do, which is dismantle the hushing of voices and histories. This framework urges educators, facilitators, and readers alike to consider the following five components:

- Uniting/Naming
- Histories
- Unlearning
- Stories
- Healing

The principles of the framework (which will be explained in detail in Chapter 2) are tools to help us use our collective power,

Figure I.2. The Principles of the un/HUSH Framework

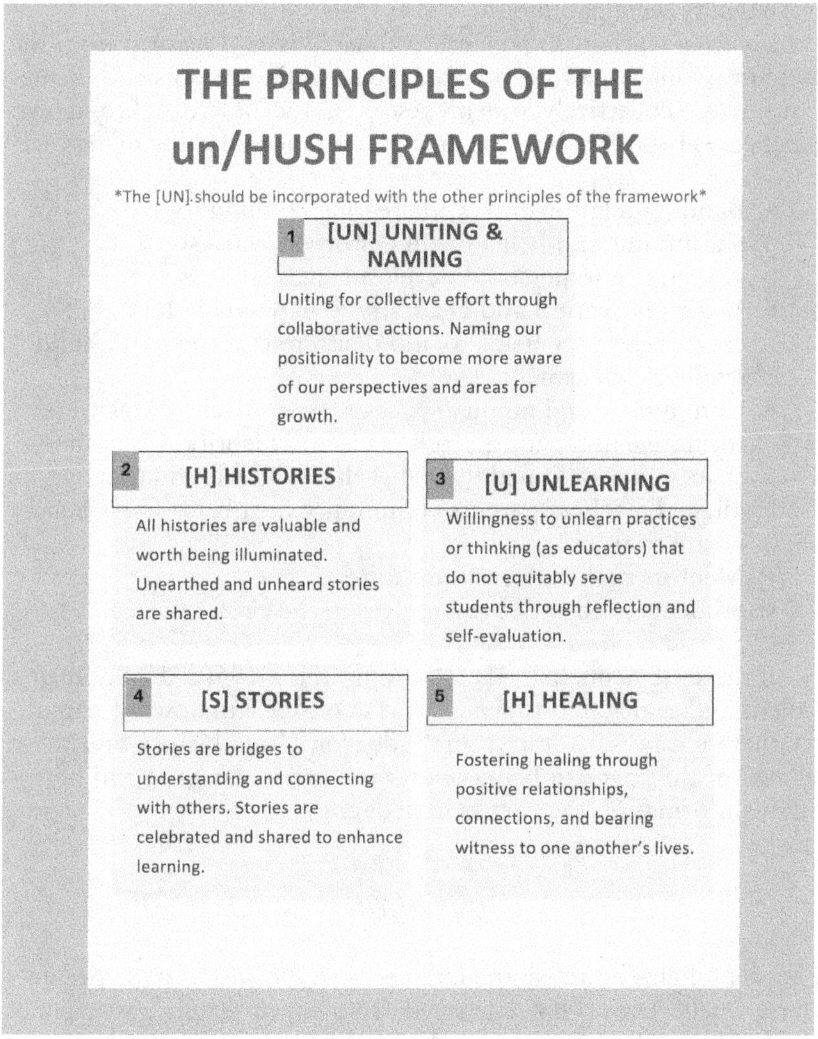

amplify voices, and incorporate culturally sustaining thinking and community immersive pedagogy into our daily practices. My participants shared with me that history, stories, and relationships allowed students to gain a sense of self despite living in a segregated world that devalued them. Dr. Ladner mentioned in the Foreword that her generation never absorbed the hush that others had, and this is a concept that I hope makes us pause for a moment to consider what an incredible feat that was, and to appreciate the fact that teaching and equality were paramount.

My own teaching experiences validated what I learned from the oral history interviews I conducted. Some of the patterns and themes that emerged collectively from my research, student feedback, and own experiences regarding best teaching practices included the following:

- Building relationships and creating community is paramount and helps sustain efforts toward students' academic and personal development.
- Using innovation and creativity to expand content and create relevancy helps to add depth to curricula and build student engagement.
- Community and affinity spaces matter. Black spaces were formative in creating Black pride and identity. Community spaces also solidified the belief that education matters and aligned teachers/parents/community members. These spaces create coalitions.
- Mentors make a significant difference.
- Students need to see themselves in the classroom.

If these elements helped classrooms in the 1950s–1970s during violent and segregated times, perhaps considering how we can apply them today is an important endeavor. Using history and these lessons of the past can help counter the curricular gaps and harmful misinformation that exists in pedagogy.

OVERVIEW

Chapter 1 helps establish the link between the past and the present. Here, I reflect on what I learned from my research participants and explore what it means to be an educator today in the wake of societal challenges. I also address how the past urges us to be a generation that works toward meaningful change.

Chapter 2 explains the un/HUSH framework in detail and discusses ideas for implementation.

Chapter 3 takes us into the action-oriented portion of the book, where you will see how to use the un/HUSH framework to help select classroom texts, plan curriculum, and craft learning activities for students. The resources in this chapter are all related to the *preplanning phase* of crafting lessons and are connected to the reflection and selection of materials and the unlearning component of the preplanning phase.

Chapter 4 segues into how to incorporate the un/HUSH framework with the arts to enhance learning. This chapter features poems from notable poets such as Claudia Rankine, Evie Shockley, Cole Swensen, Mary Ruefle, Ashley Jones, and others and features advice from poets regarding best practices when teaching poetry. I offer guidance regarding how you can use these works in your classroom to grow your culturally responsive teaching practice.

Chapter 5's purpose is to encourage the practice of honoring student voice and knowledge, which is one vital aspect of building community within the classroom. For many aspects of this chapter, I queried former students to solicit their feedback and recommendations for educators.

The Epilogue brings the text to a close and reminds us of *sankofa* (looking back and fetching what has been forgotten). As you move from chapter to chapter, remember that every story and resource is there to offer support in this meaningful work we do.

Finally, Appendices A–F offer additional resources that support equity-centered teaching and will help with the *implementation and post lesson phases* of instruction. Among other resources, here you will find lesson plan examples that were created collaboratively with educators.

Book Features

You will find that each chapter begins with the chapter title in another language (a reminder of language diversity and needs in our classrooms) and an epigraph. I use the terms *marginalized* and *Black/Brown* when referring to students and/or communities of color. Marginalized reminds us of the impact that inequitable systems, policies, and practices have created for people. Black/Brown celebrates people of color globally. Each chapter concludes with a Preservice Teacher Guidance section and a Pause and Reflect section, with a list of questions highlighting areas where you are invited to pause, put paper to pen, reflect, and engage.

While I certainly do not have answers to all the concerns we must address in education, I know for certain that collective effort and collaboration are critical. Each chapter in this book involved collaboration to represent many voices and perspectives: fellow educators, poets, artists, former students, community members, and current students. I want to elevate and share as many perspectives as possible with you.

Some of the content will be new, some might be review, but together I hope you see the blending of emerging best practices, thoughtful resources, and new approaches to help broaden and add to what already works for you. I hope this book serves as a North Star when you need it most.

The Content Areas

The lessons and references you will encounter center on English Language Arts (ELA), History, and Social Studies, as I have chosen to focus primarily on my content areas of expertise. This is important because literacy is paramount and at the core of all subjects. The resources and framework, however, are interdisciplinary and intended for use with any subject or grade level. Lastly, it is important to note that the lessons offered in Appendix C were all created in collaboration with educators in the stated grade levels and then tested in the educators' classrooms using the un/HUSH framework.

WHO SHOULD READ THIS BOOK?

While this book is for *all* educators and adults who work with students, it has aspects meant especially for preservice teachers. I recall as a new teacher wishing that I had applicable ways to incorporate the many aspects of teaching that I knew mattered. Reading this book will help new teachers feel more prepared when taking on the task of creating culturally responsive classrooms, and the close of each chapter has a dedicated section for preservice teachers. Part of equity work often overlooked is the support and guidance we offer to preservice and new educators. In that sense, this book is my way to help fill in that gap and offer something for incoming educators.

This guidebook and framework are intended to benefit students and help educators create culturally responsive lessons that allow students to feel seen and valued, and establish classrooms that are collaborative and celebratory of all cultural histories. Good teaching, cultural responsiveness, and cultural and community immersion benefit everyone and positively impact the lives of students and our craft as educators.

The title of this book, which draws on a line from a Gwendolyn Brooks poem ("we are each other's magnitude and bond"), is fitting because while writing, I realized that breakthrough moments in education happen when we are learning *together* in a community—all of us floundering, questioning, and finding ourselves through and with each other. Working collaboratively with students creates a sense of great possibility.

* * *

"Let us not forget, ever forget such things" is a quote from author Carole Maso that I have returned to time and time again throughout my life. I appreciate its message to acknowledge memory and its quiet reminder to consider how memories build our journeys. In this book, I invite you to join me as we do just that—we will recall, reflect, and use lessons of the past to inform our understanding of the future. Let's begin.

PRESERVICE TEACHER GUIDANCE

To All Aspiring Teachers,
Thank you for choosing to make teaching your career. We need you, and so do future students. Teaching is beautiful and hard. There will be times during your career when you will be exhausted and wonder why you chose this field. There will be times when you will feel underappreciated. During these moments, I hope this guidebook offers a small measure of support and appreciation for the work you are embarking on. You are not alone in this journey.

PAUSE AND REFLECT

- What is your origin story?
- Begin considering your positionality. What are your thoughts and questions related to it?
- What were your experiences as a student throughout your own schooling?

- What aspects of your family and/or neighborhood growing up shaped who you are?
- What gems or wisdom did you take from your college experiences into your classroom as a teacher?
- How will you leverage collaboration to support your journey as a novice/veteran educator and make your teaching impactful for students?

Learning From the Past to Inform Our Future

Kujifunza kutoka kwa Zamani ili Kufahamisha Mustakabali Wetu (Swahili)

> If I fall, I'll fall five feet four inches forward in the fight for freedom.
>
> —Fannie Lou Hamer

On August 28, 1955, a 14-year-old boy named Emmett Till—wide smile, bright eyes, beautiful face under the brim of his hat—was on a visit with his family in Mississippi, having left his home in Chicago for the first time. After being accused of offending Carolyn Bryant in her family's grocery store, he was abducted, tortured, and killed. He would have been 83 years old this year (Anderson, 2017; Mace, 2014).

Dr. Joyce Ladner has often spoken about being part of the "Emmett Till generation" and about the way in which that moment in history sparked a lifelong commitment to advocating for justice. It became the catalyst and reason that many of her generation became teachers and advocates for the freedom struggle. That day would create lifelong advocacy.

Though not a part of the Emmett Till generation, I consider myself a part of the Trayvon Martin generation, the Tamir Rice generation, and the collective stories of those lost to racial violence. We all have a person or moment in history that defines our generation and resonates with us in a manner that strikes us to the core. We are all part of these stories by proxy and pain.

The very same date of Emmett Till's murder, August 28, marks two other important moments in history: August 28, 1963, with the March on Washington, and then August 28, 2008, with President Barack Obama winning the nomination for president. The date of Emmett Till's death was reclaimed for moments of solidarity and joy (CBS News, 2016). History is not linear, and Black history is more than just tragedy or a singular emotion. The Emmett Till generation knew that fighting for justice meant the ebb and flow of emotion and progress. The generation who read of his murder and saw the pictures of him in the newspaper vowed to do something to make certain that such a tragedy was prevented from happening again (Ladner, 2012; Sellers, 2013; and others). They knew that this was the clarion call to invest time and energy into healing the world, and by paying homage to Emmett's memory, they would work tirelessly for change. Today, we have that same clarion call. The time is now. Effective, student-centered, culturally responsive teaching is one of the ways to answer this urgent call (Hammond, 2015; Ladson-Billings, 2014, 2022; Love, 2020).

I tell this story to set the foundation for the work that lies ahead of us. Today, we are called to remember and document lives and moments by living our own lives with a purpose that will shift this world toward justice. We work on improving education so that we can foster a world that leans on learning and love rather than hatred and false beliefs. We learn about the past to better inform our future, and so the histories shared in previous pages bring us to this moment where we examine the present.

History is always finding a way to make its presence known through patterns of recurrence. This is why bringing lessons of the past into spaces with our students, offering them further historical and social context, is imperative. Figure 1.1 offers a summary of some of the lessons gleaned from past educators during my research. They are all aspects of pedagogy that participants referenced as being foundational aspects of their pedagogy.

IMMERSIVE PRACTICES

Learning from Dr. Joyce Ladner about the ways efforts in the 1960s were amplified through collective action offers an important lens for better understanding the value of collaboration. The March on Washington and Freedom Summer, for example, occurred because people wanting to join the civil rights movement were physically present—they were in Mississippi, on the ground, doing the work alongside the community members. Together, everyone worked in a manner termed as "bottom-up organizing," living and immersing themselves within the community. Accountability and cultural responsiveness become innate when you are *in community* and *in*

Figure 1.1. Lessons of the Past

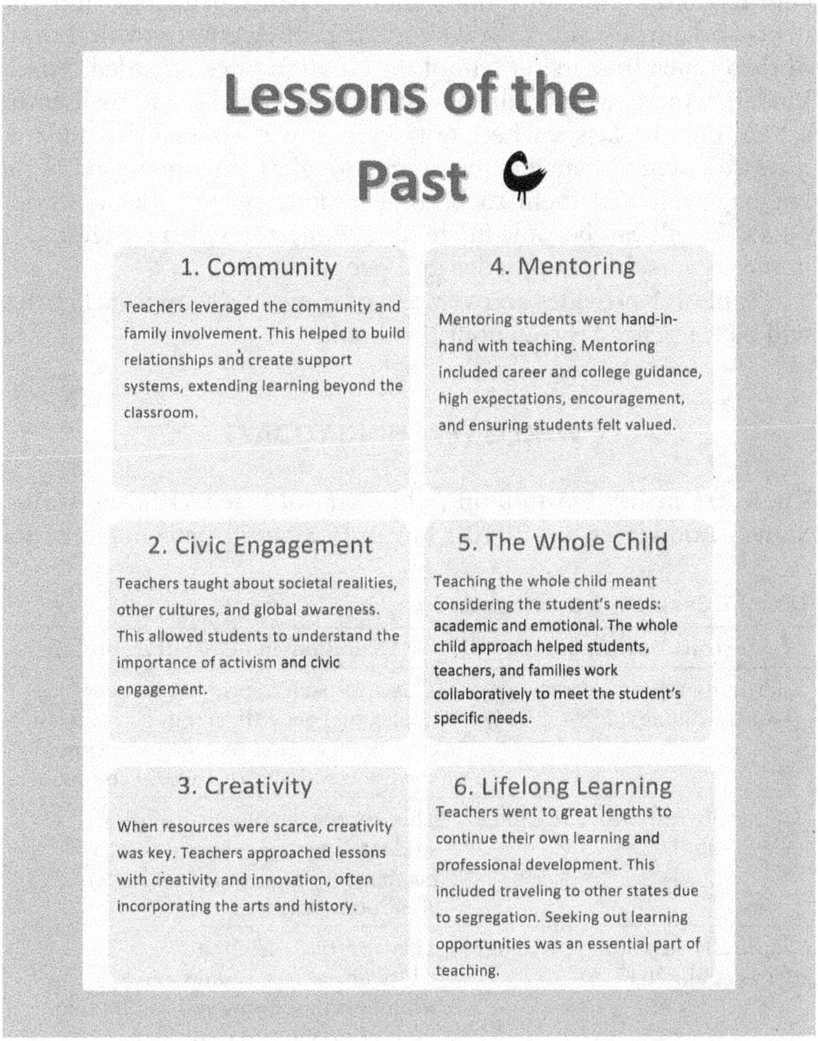

proximity to the culture and/or group you are wanting to learn about and support. It is difficult to learn about a culture or group of people from afar—you must immerse yourself in the lives of those you want to learn about, not as a tourist, but as a collaborator (Ladner, 1995; Ladner, 2000).

As educators, we need to have firsthand knowledge about the communities from which our students come. In that light, extending our thoughts about cultural responsiveness one step further—to cultural and community immersion—benefits pedagogy and students and curtails short-lived efforts regarding equity work. I think of the French immersion school my children once attended. Young kindergartners, with no fluency in French, would spend their entire school day in classes where only French was spoken. I wondered how they would manage but, soon enough, being immersed in the language allowed them to become practicing and fluent participants. We all can become fluent and connected when we choose to immerse ourselves in practice and people.

Table 1.1 provides an overview of some of the approaches that will be referenced throughout this book.

WHO IS TEACHING TODAY?

There are nearly 3.5 million public school teachers in the United States (Ludwig et al., 2010), but only a small percentage of the

Table 1.1. Culturally Responsive Approaches

Instructional Approach	Definition and Goal of Approach
Culturally relevant pedagogy (Ladson-Billings, 1994, 2014)	This approach focuses on students' intellectual growth, creating an affirming environment, and teaching students to solve societal and real-world concerns.
Culturally responsive teaching (Gay, 2000)	This approach commits to using students' customs, experiences, and perspectives as a means for better classroom practices.
Culturally sustaining pedagogy (Paris et al., 2017)	This approach celebrates multiculturalism and decenters whiteness in schools and asserts that these efforts must be sustained throughout a student's schooling.
Historically responsive literacy (HRL) (Muhammad, 2023)	This is an approach that constructs an equity framework that blends histories, identities, and literacy to create culturally responsive classrooms.
Culturally and community immersive pedagogy (Bunch, 2023)	This approach extends the practices of cultural responsiveness through community/cultural engagement and immersion.

teaching workforce is comprised of teachers of color: Black (7%), Latina/Latino/Latinx (9%), Asian American (2%), and American Indian (less than 2%) (National Center for Education Statistics, 2010). "Prior to the *Brown* decision, there were over 82,000 Black teachers in the workforce, but by 1970, more than 38,000 Black educators had lost their jobs" (Hudson & Holmes, 1994, p. 388). Between 1984 and 1989, more than 35,000 *Black* teacher candidates were screened out of the teaching profession due to certification and preparation program requirements (Fairclough, 2007; Hudson & Holmes,1994). As our student population continues to diversify, students need to see themselves in learning spaces. Having "windows, mirrors, and sliding glass doors" allows students to see themselves, bear witness to other perspectives, and immerse themselves in worlds and cultures other than their own (Hines & Hines, 2020; Hyland, 2005; Sims Bishop, 1990). Diversity cannot be abstract, therefore *seeing* representation in classrooms matters as much as having a diverse and inclusive curriculum (Ball & Tyson, 2011; Navarro et al., 2016; Perry, 2020). As Gholdy Muhammad (2023, p. 33) reminds us, "Equity is teaching and learning that is centered on justice, liberation, truth, and freedom, that is free of bias and favoritism." Equity and culturally responsive teaching involve curriculum, our teaching population, preservice education, and policy/systemic change. The ultimate goal of providing "windows, mirrors, and sliding glass doors" will require much work and our continued and collaborative efforts.

Teachers remain underpaid, overextended, and devalued. In addition to these factors, teachers of color often experience racial fatigue and workplace trauma and thus do not remain in the profession (Kohli, 2019, and others). If we want to remedy this reality, we must understand the history that has led to this situation. We must begin implementing equitable teaching practices that are more than performative. We must broaden course offerings to include culturally responsive curriculum. And we must ensure that preservice teachers are adequately supported, mentored, and educated about teaching practices that best cultivate the talents and curiosities of students and tend to the needs of our students of color (Dantas, 2007; Gay & Kirkland, 2003; Gere et al., 2009).

As our classrooms become increasingly diverse, there is a need to understand the many benefits of that diversity (Ahmad & Boser, 2014; McAllister & Irvine, 2000; Villegas & Irvine, 2010). If we can better understand systemic and historical impediments, then we can leverage unlearning and reflection to create more equitable outcomes. By listening to the stories of the past, we can better understand and inform our future approach toward inclusive classrooms and equitable educational experiences for students and their learning.

The Need to Illuminate Voices

Research has shown us that people from groups who have been historically marginalized are at risk—specifically, students and educators of color (Kohli, 2018; Kohli & Pizarro, 2016; Ingersoll & May, 2016; and others). There are risks of racial battle fatigue, racial trauma, lack of access to resources, racism, disparities in academic expectations, unfair discipline, and so on. This is not new information, but I want to offer a snapshot of the data to help us better understand the need to illuminate marginalized histories. To reverse the trend of the data from the National Center for Education Statistics (NCES) reported below, our classrooms must embrace practices that help to dismantle inequities (Albert Shanker Institute, 2015; Lewis, 2001; Richmond, 2012).

- School segregation has returned to 1968 classroom levels, even though our nation continues to diversify. This illustrates the great divide and racial mismatch in classrooms.
- Black preschoolers are 3.5 times more likely to receive one or more out-of-school suspensions. Black students are twice as likely to be expelled.
- 80% of U.S. teachers are white, but only 47% of all public elementary and secondary students in the United States are white. We know that our AAPI, Latinx, and Black student population is growing quickly (NCES, 2023).

A brief glimpse at these data shows that justice-centered spaces are needed to close the gap regarding educational disparities and the racialized experiences students are subjected to. Research has shown that culturally responsive teaching benefits a student's performance, attendance, engagement, and self-identity—specifically for students of color (Bonilla et al., 2021; Sleeter & Zavala, 2020).

Research also has indicated that educators struggle in implementing and utilizing inquiry-based teaching methods, cultural competency, and approaches to teaching histories, which hinders students' potential for achievement (Abd-El-Khalick et al., 2004). These gaps prevent students from having authentic learning experiences, which creates additional disparities for students already struggling with systemic inequities. Dismantling these inequities and building classrooms that are culturally responsive and community immersive must include honing our skills regarding the above-mentioned gaps and becoming aware of our own positionality, which can improve learning outcomes and school experiences for students. This means there is work to be done on our part if we hope to improve how we implement these useful strategies. See Figure 1.2 for ways to avoid common teaching pitfalls while working toward a culturally competent classroom.

Both/And

I recently shared a conversation with a colleague about the fear built around doing or saying the wrong thing related to equity

Figure 1.2. Roadmap to Avoid Teaching Pitfalls

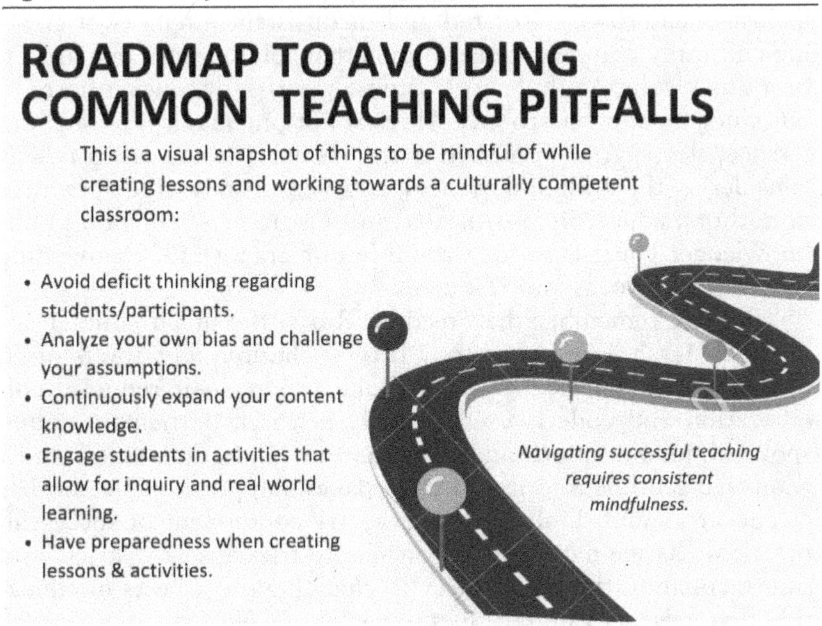

work and incorporating cultural competency in the classroom. That fear, coupled with the inundation of approaches in education, can create trepidation about which approach is best and how to implement new practices in learning spaces. When time and resources are limited, and our energy is low, which one of the many approaches do we focus on?

- Diversity/equity/inclusion (DEI)?
- Trauma-informed practices?
- Antibiased/antiracist (ABAR) teaching practices?
- Social/emotional/learning (SEL)?

Keep in mind that nothing needs to be done in isolation and that teaching practices can be tailored to be a conglomeration of many aspects of the wisdom and tools that exist. Sometimes the answer is a medley.

Adopting a both/and mindset prevents us from freezing for fear of doing the wrong thing and invites us to consider a multitude of practices that all seek the end result of equitable learning. Instead of thinking in extremes and binaries, I hope we will always consider the both/and that exists to connect ideas and practices. It takes a myriad of good teaching tools, texts, and curricula to create inclusive classrooms. Isolated and inconsistent attempts at creating culturally competent classrooms that rely on only one aspect, or a quick solution, fall short or pose the risk of causing harm to our students and classrooms. There is not one magical book, conference, strategy, or approach that does everything, which is why considering the both/and matters. Drawing from various practices of authors, educators, historians, and researchers helps build our knowledge. There is enough room in our practice for the melding of many great ideas and resources.

Do you remember the Freedom Rides, the lunch counter sit-ins, the March on Washington? It took children and adults of all backgrounds to lock arms and make progress—it required collaboration and collective efforts. My research participants often spoke about the importance of coalitions and community, and I want that sentiment to live in these pages. Supporting one another as educators and thinkers is a necessary component of successful practices. As we navigate the various restrictions of districts and states, collaboration will be key to changing the aspects of education that need reform. (See Figure I.1.)

Drivers: Actionable Pieces That Move Things Forward

Classroom drivers shape how we build and interact with our classroom and students. They are purposeful in helping us build intentionality in our work, and they help anchor our actions to the end goals we want for our learning spaces. Drivers are the actions that embody our teaching philosophies and core values. While our teaching philosophy can be broader and more expansive, drivers are more focused and ideally help us begin to think through our positionality. (Positionality is our lens and the way we view the world based on our upbringing, our beliefs, and our perspectives.)

As an educator, my work is grounded in the five drivers described below. I invite you to consider and commit to these as the anchors for this book:

1. **Create Welcoming Learning Spaces:** We will create learning spaces that are welcoming and that serve the best interests of students, families, and the community. These spaces will allow people to feel valued for who they are while learning in a space that enables each student to reach his or her highest potential. We will create spaces of joy that foster the discovery of self.
2. **Create Meaningful Connections:** We commit to fostering connections, relationships, collaboration, and coalitions by engaging with others to increase trust, learning, and perspective-taking through involvement and opportunities to connect with one another. We will bridge learning with the beloved communities of our students.
3. **Support and Expect Accountability:** We will create a culture of high expectations, inquiry, and curiosity through emerging best practices, consistency, and collaboration. We will foster the repair of grief and trauma, cultivate spaces that allow for conversations and discoveries, offer opportunities to learn, and consistently engage in unlearning/relearning/learning, to prioritize lifelong learning and reflection. We will remember that students do not need saving; they merely need believers.
4. **Engage in Purposeful and Intentional Lifelong Learning:** We know that unlearning and relearning impact our practice. We will engage in purposeful and intentional learning that offers opportunities for growth. We will

check our bias and fill in gaps in our own learning. We will be mindful of our positionality. We will research, measure our progress, track data, discuss, reflect, analyze, and implement practices aligned with the hope of creating positive outcomes for students. We will use our classroom to build community.

5. **Advocate for Civic Engagement and Community Immersion:** We will help students be advocates and stewards of the community and society—engaged and informed both locally and globally. We will demonstrate this through our own leadership and willingness to use our voices and "unlearn the hush" of accepting systems and outcomes that are not equitable. Advocating for justice and equity at a societal level will involve understanding history, systemic issues, and current events. We will guide our students toward a better understanding of information, events, history, and communities. We will make space for discussions and inquiry-based learning. We will offer opportunities to connect with students/families/communities. We will strive for equitable and inclusive practices.

Creating your own drivers is an activity that will help you synthesize what drives your classroom and help you better understand what guides your teaching. Take a moment to consider the questions below and begin drafting your own classroom drivers. Remember, drivers are your philosophies that center your work, and they should be paramount when asking yourself if your work in the classroom is aligned with your core goals and beliefs. Once you have answered the questions below, you can use those answers to create statements that embody your core goals and beliefs—your drivers (similar to the ones I shared above). These can be posted in your classroom or used as a tool for anchoring your pedagogical practices.

- What kinds of learning space(s) or classrooms are you committed to creating?
- What kinds of connections and interactions do you envision? How will you create meaningful connections and relationships?
- What will support and accountability look like in your classroom and/or learning space?

- What will intentional learning look like in your classroom, and how will you know it is occurring?
- How will you make space and listen to the voices of your students and their families? How does your positionality impact how you view and interact with your students?
- What will you advocate for? What are you willing to lose or give up in bringing this advocacy to fruition? How will you advocate for students? What will you teach your students about advocacy and equity work?

The Reality for Educators

In the wake of societal challenges today, educators are faced with so much. Today, we are grappling with book banning, teacher burnout, racial mismatch in classrooms, school violence, racial battle fatigue, restrictions regarding the accurate teaching of history, teacher shortages, poor school leadership, and much more. Educators are in the difficult position of having to navigate district and school policies, state mandates, and the fear of repercussions if these enacted norms are not adhered to. The fear of losing one's job is an ever-present reality, particularly for educators who advocate for equitable and inclusive education. Teaching, at times, feels less like an art and more like a balancing act of agendas, policies, and politics. This has not only created fear, but also reduced the freedom and creativity that allow educators to thrive. In addition, we are shouldered with the responsibility of not only educating students, but also doing so in a culturally responsive way. So, how do we go about all of this? If there is any answer, or place to begin, it is most certainly together.

LEARNING FROM OTHER EDUCATORS

The lessons of the past help us to consider histories and stories as a foundation for best teaching and learning practices for educators, practitioners, researchers, and students. The stories that inspired this book and the un/HUSH framework illustrate the deep commitment to education and students that existed in the one-room schoolhouses and communities in Hattiesburg, Mississippi. For example, Mr. Charles Cooper, who taught elementary school and college in Hattiesburg for 27 years, shared stories of how proud he was to have grown up with the teachers he had:

> Black female teachers served as role models and advisors. My role models were Mr. and Mrs. Fowler. He and his wife were both teachers who impacted the lives of so many students. The teachers cared, showed concern, and I felt like they cared for me as an individual.

He described his education as one that inspired and molded him.

Dr. Joyce Ladner shared her stories of being in segregated classrooms, of helping lead an NAACP (National Association for the Advancement of Colored People) youth chapter in Hattiesburg, of being mentored by American civil rights activist Medgar Evers, and of her work in organizing the March on Washington:

> What we didn't have in resources, our teachers made up for by dedicating their time, expertise, and mentorship.

Her tenacity and journey illustrate the change that can occur when one believes in education and lives a life dedicated to justice.

Mrs. Dolores Goins, an educator for more than 31 years, shared her wisdom and love, her teaching stories demonstrating her dedication to learning. Having been denied entry into several colleges that would not accept Black students, she worked diligently to find a college where she could gain acceptance (obtaining her bachelor's degree at Alcorn State University and master's degree at William Carey University):

> I chose to become a teacher because I had great teachers growing up in Hattiesburg. Teachers like Mrs. Heath and Mrs. Jackson were the reasons I wanted to be a teacher. They were determined that you were going to learn.

The inspiration from these stories was poured into the un/HUSH framework. That is legacy. That is the power of mentorship. I was standing among giants during my research—the greats, the changemakers—and I have never felt prouder or more empowered to be linked to these histories.

Without resources, without adequate school buildings, and without adequate funding, Black educators in Hattiesburg, Mississippi, produced self-assured, successful, bright students even when the odds were stacked against them. They were utilizing social emotional learning, trauma-informed approaches, and culturally responsive teaching before we ever had names for them. When I consider what is at the core of life-changing teaching, I think of all the stories I have collected, the stories of the past, and the stories from my own teaching.

We have histories and past efforts that built a legacy worth continuing and striving toward. Educators have historically navigated the task of resolving classroom and societal struggles, and now is no different. The time is now to reclaim our humanity, our schools, our future, and to create classrooms that allow students to feel valued and celebrated. We cannot stop advocating for policy changes, attending school board meetings, voting in every single election, and connecting with each other to better understand how to create actionable ways to implement change. Every major part of our life is in some manner connected to education: the sustainability of neighborhoods, the economy, the growth of future generations, the overall knowledge of our citizens. The promise of freedom and of a thriving future hinges on making certain that education is equitable and enriching for all students and communities. After all, education was to be the great equalizer—a symbol to the world that possibility exists for all children and students. It is time to finally make good on that promise. It is time for becoming and remaining unhushed.

There are so many things our classroom spaces need right now: cultural competency, diversity, equity, trauma-informed teaching, and more. What if we rely on the practices that were effective even during times of complete social unrest? I wanted to find a teaching framework that encompassed elements of the best pedagogical practices while also connecting classrooms to the lessons and stories of past educators. I believe that the principles of the un/HUSH framework encapsulate these practices.

Preservice Teacher Guidance

Teaching is a way to improve society. If you can teach your students to be civically engaged and understand their role in bringing about societal change, you will have achieved an important aspect of education. Past educators taught their students about the importance of voting, protesting, volunteering, and standing up for what was right. How will you do this for your students? What do you want them to learn about in regard to becoming civic beings? How can you use the classroom space to extend education that will help them navigate society and the world? What recent societal moments do you need to have a more robust understanding of that might impact the lives of your students? How can you infuse history and current events into your classroom? Offer students the chance to evaluate their thoughts around community events or societal events. Whether through journaling or small-group discussion, you can offer students the chance to explore issues that will impact their rights and their world. What do students need to know to be invested in our tomorrow?

You can model all of these things and help create students who will leave your classroom better prepared to enter the world. Always remember that you are not alone as an educator. Ask for help when you need it, and find people who will support you in your teaching journey.

I have no doubt that you will inspire the next generations of changemakers!

PAUSE AND REFLECT

- What defining generational or societal moment allowed you to recognize the importance of equity work?
- Who inspires you to teach, to transform, and to guide others? What lessons or advice have you gained from those people? How can you use their lessons in your classroom?
- As an educator and/or mentor, what legacy do you hope to create?
- What cultural or historical competency might you hope to obtain?
- How do you remain connected and civically engaged in your community and world?
- What role do stories and/or histories play in your life?
- What are the risks or downsides of deciding not to implement culturally responsive pedagogy?

Unpacking the un/HUSH Framework

un/HUSH フレームワークの解凍 (Japanese)

> Life is not what you alone make it. Life is the input of everyone who touched your life and every experience that entered it. We are all part of one another.
>
> —Yuri Kochiyama

As emphasized in Chapter 1, this book and framework carry forward the vision of past educators and activists as they worked to create equitable classrooms and visibility for marginalized histories, stories, and people. The lessons of the past help us to consider histories and stories as a foundation for best teaching and learning practices for educators, practitioners, researchers, and students. My hope is that this book will empower you to understand and elevate voices, stories, and histories that are all too often overlooked or forgotten and to use those stories as a guide toward healing and connection.

WHAT IS THE UN/HUSH FRAMEWORK?

The un/HUSH framework (Figure 2.1) was born out of my teaching experiences, my educational training and learning, and my doctoral research on Black female educators. The research I conducted made evident the great contributions and benefits that teachers of color bring to the classroom (Ahmad & Boser, 2014; Villegas & Irvine, 2010). The silence created around these women's histories can be applied to a larger issue impacting classrooms today. Whose stories do we acknowledge? What perspectives do we overlook? Who has autonomy and access? How can we listen more effectively to our

Figure 2.1. The un/HUSH Framework Overview

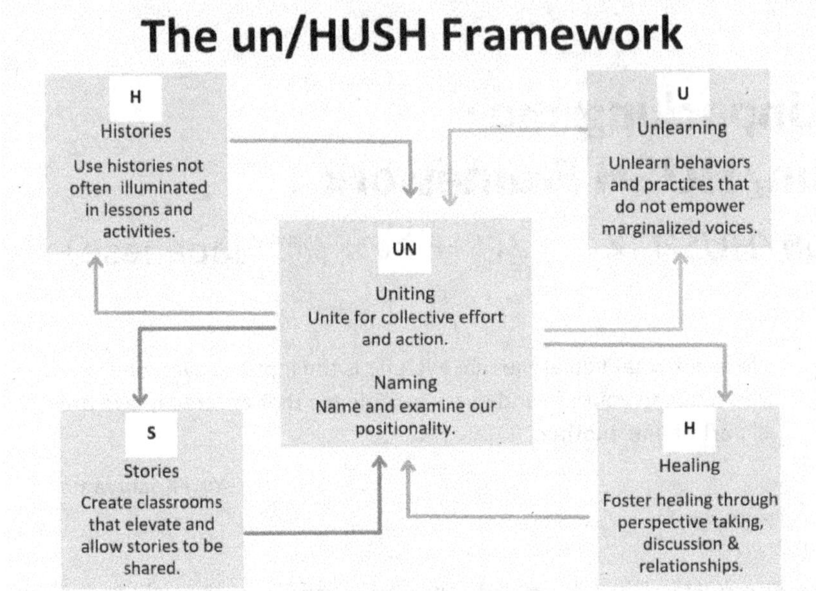

students? Most importantly, how can educators ensure that historically marginalized students feel safe and valued in learning spaces so that all students can collectively thrive? The un/HUSH framework seeks to help you and your students explore these questions and lay the groundwork for a learning space that strives toward equitable outcomes and is collectively stronger through the sharing of perspectives.

The Foundational Components

The framework urges educators, facilitators, and readers alike to consider the following five components: Uniting/Naming, Histories, Unlearning, Stories, and Healing. Implementing the framework requires us to understand the foundational aspects of the components that make up its objectives. As we think through each principle, consider ways to implement each in your lessons and activities. As you read, brainstorm ways that you might bring each principle to life in your own classroom. You can always visit my website at https://www.marleebunch.com for additional information or to reach out for support.

(UN) Uniting and Naming

Uniting for collective effort and change, as well as naming our positionality, are necessary beginning steps to the primary principles of the framework. As educators, we understand the importance of collaborative effort and coalitions. We also examine and reflect about our own positionality and how it impacts our lessons, students, and classroom. We realize that this component is not always a part of our curricula but applies in our reflection and day-to-day practices. These are two aspects of the framework that help enhance the other principles of the framework. While they may look different for each educator and classroom, these two elements can enhance your lessons and classrooms, as they activate self-reflection and collaboration with others.

(H) Histories

Use histories not often known or illuminated, which inform our teaching practices and serve as guideposts for our reflection and continued learning. Implement practices that foster histories, including the following examples: teaching historical moments, oral histories, and texts that center traditionally marginalized voices and histories to enrich our students and curricula (Dutt-Doner et al., 2016; Muhammad, 2023). As Charles Beard noted, when teaching history "we hold a damn dim candle over a damn dark abyss."

Histories should offer learning about communities and marginalized groups that are often left out of the discourse. Teaching nondominant histories and cultural narratives helps to dismantle and counter the idea that some stories are less significant than others (Wineburg et al., 2007). Consider what you wished you had learned earlier in school or life. What are some historical elements or figures not widely known, but that have been formative in shaping our world? Any state standards can be made to easily fit under this umbrella of historical or societal content. For example, if you know you need an assignment for a persuasive writing standard, have students listen to speeches by historical figures who are not widely known (e.g., Frederick Douglass and Sojourner Truth), then have students compare and contrast the perspectives by writing a persuasive essay about which elements of the speeches were most impactful to helping bring about change during that time period. This is what applying histories to a lesson might look like. In doing this, you are exposing students to two people and histories that are not widely understood or acknowledged in classroom spaces. It is also important to teach the historical context and broader understanding so that these principles are threaded throughout content and not used in isolation.[1]

(U) Unlearning

Unlearn behaviors and practices that do not center and empower voices that have been traditionally marginalized due to systemic racism and inequitable policies. Unlearn the idea that Black and Brown stories only involve trauma and require saviorism (learn about the joy and self-reliance that exist in these stories, too). Implement practices that aid in the process of unlearning. Journaling, community immersion, conversations, continuous education, practicing mindfulness, evaluating our bias, and self-work can contribute to unlearning thinking and behaviors that may negatively impact students.

Self-reflection and evaluation are important to better our practices and advance personal growth. Maria Luiza Dantas, assistant professor in the Learning and Teaching Department of the School of Leadership and Education Sciences at the University of San Diego, explains:

> The complex and rich intersection between school and family/community practices requires that teachers become "cultural brokers" in order to bring the diversity of students' and families' funds of knowledge into the learning/teaching process. Taking up an ethnographic perspective helps teachers develop new lenses for seeing and talking about the patterns and practices of life within classrooms, communities, and families, and making visible the ways in which individual lenses differ and shape what each person is able to see, interpret and come to understand. (Dantas, 2007, p. 79)

In order to become "cultural brokers," educators must first unlearn misperceptions or bias that might skew their ability to teach in an antiracist and equitable manner.

Unlearning requires two very critical elements:

1. Our own self-reflection and self-assessment
2. Continued personal and professional development

This will allow educators to craft lessons that demonstrate to students the importance of consistent unlearning, consideration of perspectives, and analysis of ideas and content. Knowing our own positionality (lens) helps us become better educators and allows us to engage in the learning process with students in an authentic and purposeful manner. Considering how a dominant narrative might skew our thoughts and ideas about students is the *prework* to any good teaching strategy. Prework is the rough-draft version of lesson planning. It is the part where we think through how the lesson or activity will benefit our students, research, take notes, gather information, engage in deep reflection, and consider intent versus impact (being mindful that good intentions do not guarantee beneficial outcomes for students).

Before creating curriculum or classroom activities, use the preplanning stage to consider questions like the following:

- What misperceptions or gaps in my own learning do I have about this topic/people?
- How can I acknowledge my own positionality and teach these histories without perpetuating bias (tourist-based pedagogy)?
- What more do I need to know regarding this topic to offer my students the most accurate information?
- Where can I go to learn more about underrepresented histories and access primary sources to gain insight into individual and historical perspectives?

There are a few ways we can help foster unlearning. Psychologist Dr. Jeff Borden suggests the following:

- *Willingness:* Willingness to see other perspectives and to acknowledge that we can always benefit from learning more.
- *Breaking Filter Bubbles:* Challenging our thinking versus reinforcing things we already believe.
- *Associative Thinking:* Approaching problems or topics from various vantage points and making connections between concepts. Seeking new opinions and ways of doing/thinking/being.
- *Change of Location:* Changing our physical location to impact how we view something.
- *Achievement of Research Saturation:* Finding credible sources, researching, following citations back to original sources, and confirming that sources are relevant and accurate. (Borden, 2021)

So, what does unlearning look like when planning for a lesson? It looks like taking time to pause and offer yourself the space to reflect, consider, research, and then unlearn and/or relearn. It is immersion into communities, articles, introspection, and so on. The unlearning element of the framework is especially for educators, but it is a component that students could also benefit from. Perhaps some of the very questions you craft to self-reflect can be shared with students as a precursor to a lesson or unit. Model examples of unlearning by taking part in the activities you are asking of your class and illustrating what you discovered through your own unlearning.

(S) Stories

Create classrooms and spaces that elevate and allow stories to be shared. Use stories as a vehicle to build rapport, connections, and community. Implement practices that allow stories to emerge and create spaces that value storytelling. Use narrative, poetry, sharing of stories, Socratic seminars, retelling of uncommon stories, writing prompts, and activities that help serve as implementation strategies to create a space where stories are celebrated and valued (Akinbode, 2013; Pacheco, 2009). Diane Ketelle, professor of education at Mills College, explains:

> By framing classroom instruction in a storytelling pedagogy, it is possible to see different, at times contradictory, layers of meaning and to bring these opposing layers into useful dialogue with one another. The process of storytelling also gives way to increased understanding of the individual and increased awareness of social justice. (Ketelle, 2017, p. 144)

Teaching diverse authors and poets not typically explored works to expand our view of stories and of whose stories matter. Some of my favorites include Claudia Rankine, Zora Neale Hurston, Toni Cade Bambara, Evie Shockley, Ta-Nehisi Coates, Ava Dellaira, Audre Lorde, Jaqueline Woodson, Toni Morrison, and a plethora of others (Ketelle, 2017). We know that literacy is important, and recent research shows that literacy and stories can offer additional benefits beyond the academic (Dutro, 2019).

Stories are the connective element that connects students to learning content. They also bridge relationships with students and allow them to connect with one other (Cron, 2012; Short, 2012). This element will allow content to become more relevant and helps move learning from rote memorization to engagement and understanding.

Stories offer choice and the ability to opt in to opportunities to share lived experiences (Ehret & Leander, 2019). Allowing stories to exist in our learning spaces creates connections from past to present, allows for student voice and autonomy to exist, and creates opportunities for inquiry and connection to occur (DeNicolo & Gonzalez, 2015; Ghiso & Low, 2013; Handsfield & Valente, 2016).

(H) Healing

Allow the opportunity for healing to occur from listening to others' perspectives, collaborating, creating accountable spaces, and building relationships (Boutte et al., 2017). The goal is to foster healing, and it is of course an ongoing process; there is no quick fix or fast solution. Implement practices that are rooted in relational teaching pedagogies (Aspelin, 2021), prioritizing the relational, community engagement pursuit of authentic inquiry with collaborative partners who have an aligned mission or shared interest. For example, research by David Hawkins emphasizes the importance of relationships and classroom interactions that occur (Hawkins, 1974/2007). Mentoring and connecting with students' families and care teams are ways to foster healing and connection (Ball & Lai, 2006).

Responsive teaching also reiterates the importance of pedagogies that foster healing and awareness of our students' needs. Educator and author Brittany Collins states:

> We can take an additive approach to curricular and cocurricular work, asking ourselves, "If we cannot get rid of students' grief or trauma, how—instead—can we supplement and counteract it? How can we make classroom communities oppositional to the stressful environments that many students endure?" (Collins, 2021, p. 11)

To create meaningful change, we must seek collective healing. And while this is a broad goal, it invites us to incorporate practices of trauma-informed care, restorative teaching tools, storytelling, affinity groups, and other best practices that support our classrooms (Nadworny, 2015). This can also include reflection, celebrating perspectives and voices, and using dialogue to process learning content. It acknowledges that pain and joy coexist—in history, in our experiences, and in classrooms. Fostering healing does not mean fixing or counseling on our part; it means creating opportunities for connection and bearing witness to our students' lives. Fostering healing includes opportunities to share perspectives that connect to our learning and the commitment to embrace pedagogical practices that support students' social and emotional well-being (Collins, 2021). Fostering healing can look different based on the needs of your students and classroom. Sometimes, healing may simply mean taking time to pause and journal, creating opportunities to process and discuss, or engaging with a text that resonates. It is important to remember that healing is a continuous process. Additionally, if a student needs resources or help beyond your scope, partner with or defer to the school counselors or social workers in your building to provide additional support. Resources offered by the Dougy Center, School Crisis Recovery & Renewal, and The National Child Traumatic Stress Network (NCTSN) all provide valuable information and sources.

IMPLEMENTATION

We know that action and application matter. Therefore, how do we begin using histories, unlearning, stories, and healing—all the principles that make up the un/HUSH framework (Figure 2.1)—in the classroom? What does it look like, and where do we start? It is worth noting that one element of a lesson or unit might satisfy two of the components of the framework; they might not always be separate. The framework can be applied while planning curricula, considering classroom activities, and choosing classroom texts, and as a guide for personal introspection or to help facilitate discussion. Let's begin by looking at the ways we might include each in our learning spaces and classrooms.

Implementing (H) Histories

Histories can include any of the components shown in Table 2.1 (and others you might brainstorm). Note that none of these suggestions should be taught or done in isolation, as illustrating the broader perspective is important. Culturally responsive and community responsive teaching should be interwoven throughout lessons and practices, avoiding singular attempts.

Sharing and celebrating histories will help you expose your students to an appreciation for history, people, and diverse backgrounds. Continuously expanding the scope for students can be done by showing them the vastness of our world and the deep and complicated history that goes with it. Sharing with them the

Table 2.1. Ideas for Implementing Histories

Idea/Topic	Example Student Activity
Biographies, autobiographies, and memoirs	Students can learn about stories of current or historical people not widely known or celebrated. This can be accomplished through books, videos, oral histories, and exhibitions.
Movements	Teach about historical movements (e.g., the women's suffrage movement, the civil rights movement, etc.) using texts, primary sources, podcasts, and videos.
Coalitions and collaborative groups	Students can evaluate historical or current-day efforts toward collective activism (e.g., grassroots organizations or historical coalitions).
Poetry, historical fiction, and flash fiction	Use creative writing (e.g., flash fiction or poetry) or historical fiction to introduce historical moments. An example: *Dear Memory* by Victoria Chang.
The history of systems, policies, and laws	Students can reimagine, rewrite, or modify historical or existing laws (e.g., housing, banking, voting, etc.) after examining their impact. Documentaries help capture these systems, policies, and so forth. For example: *College Behind Bars*, *The Pruitt-Igoe Myth*, *13th*, or *Amend: The Fight for America*.
Stories and oral histories of changemakers	Students can listen to an oral history online at the Library of Congress, Smithsonian, or Oral History Association. Additional primary or secondary sources can be used for further context.
Artifacts (historical objects) and/or historical documents	Students can examine photographs, letters, maps, newspapers, diaries, or speeches.
Historical sites, museums, monuments, and memorials	Students can visit historical sites and markers in person or virtually to gain deeper historical knowledge. Students can examine the impact of a particular monument or memorial.

historical and lived experiences of people in conjunction with historical moments will offer them the benefit of humanizing history.

Challenge yourself to shine a light on atypical events and people. Classrooms and textbooks often teach the proverbial topics and names. Try to discover people and things not commonly taught or widely known. (Table 2.2 includes a few suggestions but is not an exhaustive list—there are vast possibilities and many more people and events to consider.)

Table 2.2. Moments/People to Consider Illuminating When Unearthing Histories

People/Topics	Background Context	Use
Vernon and Ellie Dahmer, Dr. Joyce and Dorie Ladner, Medgar Evers, Bob Moses	People who worked toward civil rights	Could be used in a history course, language arts course, or civics course
Grace Lee Boggs, Emma Gee, Yuji Ichioka, George Takei, Larry Itliong, Mary Matsuda	AAPI individuals who helped with civil and AAPI rights	Could be used in a history course, writing course, or language arts course
John Herrington, Ben Nighthorse Campbell, Ira Hayes	Notable Native American individuals	Could be used in a history course or ELA course
Celia Cruz, Nina Simone, Gordon Parks, and many others. Explore the role of music and art in history.	Artists from various backgrounds and art media	Could be used in an art course, history course, music course, or ELA course
Freedom Schools/ Freedom Summer	1960s/civil rights history	Could be used in a history course, writing course, or literature course
Authors/artists/poets (historical or current-day)	Any time period or person that is applicable	Could be used in any course
Student Non-Violent Coordinating Committee (SNCC)	Black history, 1960s history	Could be used in a history course, social studies course, or ELA course
Black codes	Black history, 1860s	Could be used in a history course, ELA course, or writing course
The history of how quilts were used in the Underground Railroad	Black history, 1830s	Could be used in a history course or ELA course
Mary McLeod Bethune, Ida B. Wells, Septima Clark, Fannie Lou Hamer	Black history, 1930s–1960s	Could be used in a history course or civics course
Rosenwald Schools	Black history	Could be used in a history course or ELA course

Note: See the 30-day challenge topics in Appendix D for additional events/people to consider. These can be applied to most courses.

Implementing (U) Unlearning

Unlearning is a core concept that makes the un/HUSH framework unique. This principle is intended specifically for you as the educator. It is intended to help you pause and consider your own perspectives as you craft lessons and implement activities. This reminder helps examine bias, consider confirmation bias, hone critical thinking, and fill in knowledge gaps. This unlearning principle is meant to be personal and powerful, and it is a space for you to better your gifts and crafts as a teacher. Though intended especially for you (the educator), you could share practices of unlearning with your students.

Taking the time to consider what you think about your students is a critical part of ensuring that an approach is successful. To have equitable results, we must unlearn misperceptions about students that might cause us to underestimate a student's abilities. Bias is insidious and finds its way into our thoughts even when we are unaware, so taking the time to pause and consider what we need to relearn is imperative in the work we do. How can we challenge ourselves to see beyond the surface of our students (e.g., grade cards, test scores, labels, etc.)? How do we prevent typecasting our students?

Table 2.3 lists a few ways to help foster the process of unlearning.

Implementing (S) Stories

Stories can help bring our classrooms and curriculum to another level. They are the glue that can create transformative moments (Cron, 2012; Fox & Short, 2003). Stories can come from anywhere, especially from our students. Remembering to include their lens, their experiences, and their voices can enhance learning. Use the stories and experiences of your students to enhance learning, create connections to learning content, and expand perspectives. Stories are bridges to understanding and connecting with others. As you facilitate students sharing stories, work to ensure a variety of stories are celebrated. The goal here is to allow students the chance to connect their own lives and lived experiences to the content from the lesson, which makes learning relevant and personal. Stories also build connections to the content and to one another, as telling our story affirms our experiences, helps us to develop empathy, and has the potential to open us up to others' perspectives and lived experiences.

Table 2.4 lists a few activities that allow stories to become an integral part of your lessons and the classroom.

Table 2.3. Activities to Foster Unlearning

Activity	Example
Journaling and written reflection	Use the reflection prompts given in Appendix E.
Self-assessment, self-evaluation, and soliciting feedback	Use the un/HUSH self-evaluation (see Appendix B, Figure B.1) and solicit feedback from colleagues, mentors, and students.
Consistently assessing your positionality/lens/bias/ misinformation, as well as knowledge gaps	Use the positionality charts in Figures 3.2 and 3.3 to help you consider various aspects of your positionality. Use journaling to reflect and process.
Engaging in lifelong learning; seeking out professional development opportunities that are aligned with your needs and goals	For example, Facing History & Ourselves offers virtual workshops and development related to various topics.
Reading, researching, and relying on credible sources to enhance your knowledge and expertise.	Sites such as the Library of Congress, Smithsonian Educator Resources, and universities offer valuable resources and information. For example, if you want to learn more about AAPI history, you can visit https://teaach.education.illinois.edu
Practicing open-mindedness and considering perspectives different from your own; creating opportunities to immerse yourself in new and different spaces	Serve as a board member for a local nonprofit, take part in a book discussion group, register for virtual or in-person workshops, or attend local cultural events (often featured through local museums and cultural centers).
Offering students opportunities to engage in their own unlearning by modeling your own thinking, learning, and unlearning as tangible examples	Model aloud for students as you work through a layered brainstorm chart about an upcoming topic or unit, journal as your students are journaling, etc.

Table 2.4. Activities That Help Stories Emerge

Activity	Examples
Student-centered learning activities and/or projects that consider student voice and lived experiences	A cento poem (see Chapter 4, Figure 4.1 for an example and Table 4.2 for guidance), a PechaKucha presentation (a format that uses 20 slides, one image per slide, images are displayed for 20 seconds; see https://www.pechakucha.com for details), an oral history project, or an I-Search. An I-Search, for example, is a great way to introduce students to research while allowing their curiosities to guide inquiry. After introducing the I-Search and its components, students choose a topic of interest, research that topic, produce an I-Search paper, and present about their topic. The project helps promote student-led inquiry and research skills. You can find additional information and resources for the I-Search online at sites such as Read Write Think: https://www.readwritethink.org/professional-development/strategy-guides/promoting-student-directed-inquiry (Lyman, 2006; Macrorie, 1998).
Writing activities	Journaling, narrative writing, bell work (short activities for 5–10 minutes at the start of class), and creative writing (see Chapter 4 for information on creative writing). For example, ask students to write for 5 minutes using a journal prompt of your choice. You might invite students to write about what part of the world they would most like to see and why. Additional prompts are offered in Chapter 5.
Research and inquiry-based activities	I-Search, oral history project, or research paper
Art-based activities	Art journals, poetry, activities that involve music or art, or video poems
Exposing students to diverse and varied authors and texts	Supplement required texts with works by diverse authors: articles, poems, op-eds, historical fiction, or excerpts from novels. A few authors to consider are Eula Biss, Zadie Smith, Michelle Zauner, Jhumpa Lahiri, Isabel Wilkerson, Sandra Cisneros, Jesmyn Ward, Christopher Span, Tiya Miles, Michelle Zauner, Elizabeth Acevedo, Colson Whitehead, Derrick Barnes, the poets listed in Table 4.3, and others.

(continued)

Table 2.4. Activities That Help Stories Emerge (*continued*)

Activity	Examples
Writing groups and collaborative activities or projects	Students can write group poems/essays, engage in feedback groups, and conduct group research. This builds community and perspectives.
Creating opportunities to present, discuss, and share ideas	Discussions, debate, Socratic seminar, jigsaw, fishbowl discussions, and presentations
Creating a *Magnitude of Us* wall in your classroom	Use white paper and let students fill it with images, words, and goals.

Implementing (H) Healing

Classrooms have the ability to foster healing, and we have much to heal from: racial trauma, grief, loss, mental health struggles, post-pandemic stresses, violence, and more. Healing is the culmination of all good things: equity, good relationships, learning, listening, discussion, and building community. Musician Townes Van Zandt shares lyrics that say, "we all got holes to fill, and them holes are all that's real." The things we have endured, and our hurt, come with us as we move from space to space. Intentionally acknowledging that those who occupy our classroom spaces come with a wide variety of experiences and griefs is important. This is not an invitation to fall into saviorism, but rather an opportunity to use learning spaces as places that foster individual and collective healing. Choosing to acknowledge trauma and grief allows us to move toward joy and love. And though healing is a lifelong endeavor, the act of moving toward the wholeness that healing provides is no doubt an important one (Collins, 2021). Trauma-informed classrooms and practices require considering the expansive landscape surrounding trauma and grief, as well as our role in that work (Goldin & Khasnabis, 2021; Venet, 2021).

Use the classroom as a space that allows for connections and relationships to support what students are experiencing. Inequities, injustice, and lived experiences involve grief, hardship, and trauma. Collective healing allows us to acknowledge that grief and joy coexist and that supporting one another opens up possibilities for tomorrow. Mindful lessons that allow students to feel seen and heard, plus positive relationships and connections, help foster healing.

Table 2.5 provides suggestions for moving toward healing. I encourage you to add to this list.

Table 2.5. Activities to Foster Healing

Suggestions	Examples
Use stories that emerge as a place for empathy and listening to grow.	Socratic seminars, fishbowl discussions, and reflective writing
Name it—name the emotional content of the climate (Collins, 2021).	Do not be afraid to directly name emotions or realities that students, or the world, are facing.
Create collaborative endeavors that connect students/teachers/community.	Invite community members to speak in your classroom, call families and caretakers to share positive news, send out newsletters or email updates, or collaborate with a colleague.
Listen, then listen harder, without judgment or the need to fix.	Listen to your students without interruption. Model and teach students what good listening entails.
Do the work of repair (whatever that means for your classroom). Create actionable solutions toward change. Take time to discover and plan how you will incorporate opportunities that foster healing in your classroom.	One-to-one conferences with students, classroom contracts and expectations, dedicated time for discussions, and clear procedures
Inform yourself about grief-responsive teaching and trauma-informed care (Collins, 2021).	Read and research to better understand how to help grieving students. *Learning From Loss* by Brittany Collins (2021) is a good text to start with.
Advocate for your students and families—always.	Attend meetings related to your students (e.g., 504 meetings, IEP meetings, etc.), attend school board meetings, and have an open-door policy to engage with families when needed.
Take care of yourself and consider your own restoration and healing.	Use your time off, avoid taking on extra tasks without additional compensation, and find ways to practice self-care.
Bear witness to the stories and experiences of others.	Listen, acknowledge, and avoid the need to rescue or fix.

(*continued*)

Table 2.5. Activities to Foster Healing (*continued*)

Suggestions	Examples
Be willing to give up comfortability. Be challenged; it usually leads to growth.	Ask questions, admit when you do not know something, acknowledge your areas for growth, engage in difficult discussions, and observe.
Create accountable and safe learning spaces. You can't guarantee safety, but you can work to maintain expectations and accountability, which leads toward establishing a sense of safety.	Create and sustain a classroom built on expectations of respect. Consistency matters.
Learn about self-care and mental health practices that can be resources for yourself and your students. Make those resources available to students and families and communicate your students' needs with school professionals (counselors, social workers) who might have additional resources. If a student needs help beyond your scope, refer them. This will work toward destigmatizing seeking help with healing and/or mental health.	Offer a list of resources in your classroom should a student or family need it. Establish collaborative relationships with school counselors and social workers.
Use lessons and wisdom from the past to guide actions that allow opportunities for healing to occur.	Listen to oral histories and stories of past educators, examine histories you do not know, and allow stories to illuminate our differences and connectedness.
Build in classroom time to check in with students one-to-one.	Create regular check-in times or mini-conferences with students.
Work to be a bridge and build relationships. Mentor. Serve as a role model.	Ask questions, learn about your students, listen, and engage.
Healing can be cultivated by many things—including joy, laughter, and celebrations. Take time to do all of these in your learning spaces with students.	Celebrate accomplishments, play music, go on field trips, find joy, laugh, and enjoy your students and classroom.
Be an advocate for equality and justice. Be civically engaged. Social consciousness matters.	Vote. Attend school board meetings. Understand the policies your school adheres to.

Now that we have walked through some guiding beliefs, data, and considerations, and have examined some of the ways that we can drive action through using histories, unlearning, stories, and healing in the classroom, let us consider how we can utilize the un/HUSH framework to create lessons and activities that will work to sustain culturally responsive classrooms. Chapter 3 offers an in-depth look at the un/HUSH framework and then segues into providing an abundance of resources to help you begin this journey.

PRESERVICE TEACHER GUIDANCE

As a future or new teacher, you will need many tools to build your practice, and that endeavor will be ongoing. I hope that the un/HUSH framework provides support for you. Think of ways you can create a buffet of your favorite practices and tools. Keep a journal to write down things that work or don't work in your classroom. Remember that teaching tools often need modification and edits to best fit our learning spaces—make those adjustments as you see fit. No one knows your classroom and your students better than you.

I asked a former student, who had just begun his first year of teaching, what he thought preservice teachers might ask about using histories/unlearning/stories/healing. Here is what he shared. Use this list to build your own questions and reflect on what you want to know more about. Use the questions to reflect, journal, and engage in discussions with your mentor/friend/colleagues. Once you know what you need to know more about, you are better equipped to know precisely what to ask for in order to receive the support and resources you need.

(H) History

- What changes have occurred throughout education (understanding where education has come from and where we are headed)? What historical aspects of education create access and equity for some but not for others?
- How does the history of education affect students? How does it affect teachers?

(U) Unlearning

- What ruts do teachers get into with negative mindsets? How can we avoid this?
- If you find yourself becoming negative, how can you unlearn this way of thinking?

(S) Stories

- What have teachers struggled with, and how did they triumph?
- Preservice teachers are often told what not to do, but they are not given the tools to recover. What tools help educators recover from mistakes?

(H) Healing

- What does trauma-informed teaching look like from a healing perspective?
- How can teachers help students begin to understand the healing process?

PAUSE AND REFLECT

- What do you want or need to know more about regarding histories/history?
- How will your own story impact your classroom and students? How will your practices and lessons center voices that have historically and/or to date been overlooked or silenced?
- How can you build your planning practices around the concepts of the un/HUSH framework? How will those practices be visible and evident?
- What do you need to unlearn/relearn?
- What aspects of healing would you like to see in your classroom?
- What might you need to heal from?
- How can teacher wellness be supported?
- What successful lessons or practices do you currently use that can be combined with the un/HUSH framework?
- What additional information or support would be helpful?

CHAPTER 3

Planning Curriculum and Learning Activities for Students

Pianificazione del curriculum e delle attività di apprendimento per gli studenti (Italian)

> In order to see where we are going, we not only must remember where we have been, but we must understand where we have been.
>
> —Ella Baker

So many times, while lesson planning, I have scrambled to find worthwhile resources that will support the endeavor of creating meaningful classroom content. Having good resources as an educator assists us in creating the best learning opportunities for students and managing the many tasks we must maintain in the classroom. The following sections are not meant to be rigid or prescriptive, but rather are intended to serve as a bright light to help guide you in times of need and through the joys, struggles, peaks, and valleys of the school year. These resources are here for you, I hope, to ease some of your load and help you feel supported. These resources will help with *preplanning*, which involves self-reflection, research, assessment of the materials you intend to use, and taking the time to share and introduce foundational information with your students. There are additional resources in the appendices, so be sure to spend some time there at the end of the book.

As discussed in Chapter 2, the un/HUSH framework recognizes the need to illuminate and teach content and material that is culturally relevant and to consistently find ways to disrupt pedagogies that do not move us toward an equitable educational system. Because all learners have different needs, the framework can be adapted as necessary for K–12 classrooms, postsecondary classrooms, gifted learners, English language learners (ELLs), and any subject or content area. The framework can also be used in conjunction with other best practices. Consistently using the framework helps us avoid the pitfalls of celebrating cultures and histories based on calendar observances or of lumping in a lesson to check off the task of employing equity in the classroom—shortcuts that can be haphazard, inconsistent, and harmful, and can appear inauthentic. Efforts toward cultural responsiveness should be authentic, embedded, and connected to other content, and should occur regularly because they are intentional and prioritized.

Through stories, snapshots of exemplary practice, teaching strategies, and reflective questions, the resources in this chapter help bring the un/HUSH framework alive while making it relevant to any classroom. Exploring the materials will help you make sense of the framework and feel comfortable using it, and will allow you the space to make personal meaning of the content.

LESSON PLANNING TEMPLATE

The lesson planning template is a tool to help in the beginning stages of planning lessons and units. The template walks you through the core components of a lesson, using the foundation of unlearning and reflection as its core. This lesson template differs from others in that it is interactive and asks you, the educator, to self-evaluate and reflect. The preplanning phase of your lessons and activities helps to prevent last-minute lessons that do not serve students well. If you are a new teacher, this template is an important tool for setting up your lesson for success.

Note that the lesson planning template (Figure 3.1) is also available as a printer-friendly 8.5 × 11-inch PDF download at https://teachers-college-press.myshopify.com/products/the-magnitude-of-us_9780807769881.

Figure 3.1. Lesson Planning Template

Lesson Planning Template

(continued)

Considering your Positionality: Have you considered your own positionality (lens)? How have you considered bias and gaps in your knowledge? What are they and how will you address them before implementing this lesson? What gaps in understanding or information might you have related to the upcoming lesson? Use this space to reflect and self-examine.

Lesson Objective(s) & Resources: State your objectives clearly, ensuring you have considered all aspects of the un/HUSH framework. What resources or materials do you need to implement the lesson?

Standard(s)/Benchmark(s): How are you aligning your lesson with state or district standards?

(*continued*)

Figure 3.1. Lesson Planning Template (*continued*)

Anticipatory Set: How are you going to engage your students...review prior knowledge...introduce your topic...organize your lesson for students... help make content relevant?

THE UN/HUSH FRAMEWORK SELF-REFLECTION GUIDE

An important aspect of teaching is self-reflection. The un/HUSH framework supports implementing lessons, content, and student-centered learning. This self-reflection guide asks you, as the educator, to engage in deep self-reflection and self-assessment. Unlearning bias or misinformation that we may hold helps to make certain that we are approaching our work as educators from a position of continuous growth and lifelong learning. Learning, unlearning, and relearning make us better educators. One of the most effective practices I have engaged with both in and out of the classroom is journaling. The questions in Tables 3.1–3.4 are here to help you as you work through your own thoughts, ideas, and processes as an educator. Feel free to modify them to best fit your specific needs. The reflection questions are scaffolded based on each component of the framework. Track your thoughts in a separate journal to document and witness your personal growth.

Table 3.1. Reflection Questions—Histories

We understand that all histories are valuable and worth being illuminated. We work to ensure that unearthed and unheard histories are shared and elevated.
1. In what ways do you use histories and oral histories to build connections and relationships to the past and present?
2. Describe what embracing the history of others looks like in your classroom.
3. What does inclusive history mean to you? How can you model inclusive teaching practices for others?
4. Describe how you share, honor, and value the identities and cultures of everyone. How will your students know this?
5. What does it look like in your classroom when you embrace and teach about histories and perspectives of marginalized people and communities?
6. What elements are necessary for a genuine understanding of silenced or unheard histories? What work will you need to do to understand those aspects?
7. How do you expand your perspectives of history and your societal/worldview?
8. In what ways are you willing to challenge your own beliefs and current knowledge about history?
9. What do you need to do in order to learn histories that you have not yet learned? What histories have been overlooked? How can you embrace these histories beyond just reading about them?
10. Do you use inquiry-based learning that allows students to experience histories and stories not often illuminated? How? Where can students see those histories in your lesson/texts/classroom activities?

Table 3.2. Reflection Questions—Unlearning

We work to unlearn tendencies that do not create equitable and inclusive learning opportunities for all students. We recognize that unlearning should be done consistently and shared with students when applicable.
1. What do you need to unlearn in order to best serve students, particularly students of color?
2. What resources do you consistently utilize when planning learning for your classroom? Are those resources dedicated and committed to antiracist and equitable outcomes for students?
3. Do you work to center and empower marginalized voices? What does that look like? Do you avoid color-evasive thinking (the sentiment that one does not see color, and denial of racial differences)?
4. What aspects of unlearning might you or your students need help with because of messages received from the media/society/systems? How can you help guide and model that unlearning?
5. What quality and reliable resources can you access to continue your personal growth?

Table 3.3. Reflection Questions—Stories

We understand that stories are bridges to understanding and connecting with others. We work to ensure that stories are celebrated and shared and that an accountable and safe space exists where these stories can emerge when students choose to share.
1. Do monuments and images of stories exist in your learning spaces? Describe one.
2. What resources do you need in order to equitably elevate stories that have not yet been heard or embraced?
3. Whose stories do you most often listen to? Whose stories have you possibly overlooked?
4. How can you incorporate stories into learning activities? What do we have to gain from stories?
5. What visuals can you utilize to foster stories and histories? Choose one that you plan to incorporate into your learning space.
6. How do visual elements connect learners to content/stories/cultures? Answering these questions may require some research on your part.
7. How can using materials, texts, and visuals that positively represent diverse identities also help develop the self-identity of yourself and your students?
8. What are the benefits of bearing witness to someone's story and perspective taking?

Table 3.4. Reflection Questions—Healing

We understand that racial inequities and injustice result in trauma and grief that require healing. We work to create an environment that is responsive in facilitating both healing and positive relationships.
1. What does it look like when a community forgives? What might you need to be forgiven for? How can you teach others to lead with an open heart?
2. How do you work toward creating an identity safe and affirming learning space?
3. If we looked at our shared past and worked to foster repair and healing, what would it look like to get there? What would it look like individually? Collectively?
4. What does empathy look like for your students? For yourself?
5. In what ways can you use education to move systems and society toward healing?
6. How can the lived experiences of others help us better understand ourselves and one another?

(*continued*)

Table 3.4. (*continued*)

7. What do you do to facilitate opportunities for healing to occur in your learning space?
8. Describe what is needed for you to challenge harmful policies, behaviors, and practices. What actions from you create a more equitable educational system?
For a printable journal to use along with the book please go to https://teachers-college-press.myshopify.com/products/the-magnitude-of-us_9780807769881. It appears at the bottom of the web page.

POSITIONALITY

Considering our positionality helps us to align our practices with the needs of our students. The chart in Figure 3.2 allows us to consider our positionality and intersectionality (Milner, 2007). Positionality is the lens through which we see the world, and intersectionality includes the ways that race/gender/class/and so on intersect and overlap to form our individual experiences. Positionality and intersectionality are aspects to be mindful of when considering ourselves, lesson planning, and interactions with students.

One of the first assignments I was given when I began my doctoral program was to write a paper about my positionality. In all my years of teaching, it was never something I had taken the time to truly reflect on. It was an assignment that greatly impacted me and allowed me to better understand not only my lens but also the myriad ways that our positionality, and those of our students, shows up in the classroom. Naming our positionality is an additional level of reflection that helps us better understand ourselves (Frost, 2019). Considering our positionality when creating lessons can be a useful tool for checking for cultural competence. It can also help avoid sentiments of color and culture evasion (the assertion of not seeing differences between cultures or color, which dismisses individual beauty and relevance). The two charts that follow are useful when reflecting, planning for a one-to-one with a student, or assessing how the learning content might interact with a student's individual background and/or needs. The first chart (Figure 3.2) offers a positionality exercise to begin delving into the concept of what our positionality entails. The second graphic (Figure 3.3) offers guidance when interacting with students or the content of a lesson. Take a moment to walk through the questions in the positionality exercise, and then see if answering those questions allows you to create a brief positionality statement.

Figure 3.2. Positionality Exercise

Positionality Exercise

POSITIONALITY: OUR PERSPECTIVE AND LENS REGARDING HOW WE VIEW AND INTERACT WITH KNOWLEDGE AND PEOPLE (COHEN & CRABTREE, 2006).

STEP 1: IDENTITY

What groups do I identify with—race, gender, culture, age, social class, ability, religion, etc.? How important is each group to my identity and my actions as an educator?

STEP 2: HISTORY

What aspects of my history have influenced who I am: my beliefs, communication, childhood, educational experiences, family, etc.? What positive and negative experiences have shaped my perspectives?

STEP 3: ROLES

What roles do I have (i.e. mother, husband, step-parent, widow, sibling, caretaker, veteran, etc.), and how do these roles impact the way that I teach and who I am?

STEP 4: BELIEF AND VALUES

What beliefs and values do I consider to be important to my identity? How do these beliefs & values show up in the classroom? How might my beliefs and values impact students? From whom, or where, did I inherit these beliefs?

STEP 5: UNLEARNING AND ACTION

What actionable steps can I take to ensure that my positionality does not create an inequitable or unjust classroom? What unlearning could benefit me?

STEP 6: REFLECT/DISCUSS

What additional questions might you consider or add? Take a few moments to reflect and/or discuss.

Figure 3.3. Considering Our Positionality

Considering Our Positionality

1. What is my ________?
   - How might my ________ influence my current perspective of this lesson's content?
   - What might I need to unlearn or relearn as a result of my ________?

2. What is the student's ________?
   - How might the student's ________ interact with the lesson?
   - What needs might there be as a result of the student's ________?

IDENTITY
LANGUAGE
SOCIOECONOMIC STATUS
GENDER IDENTITY
VETERAN FAMILY STATUS
PERSONALITY TYPE
AGE
HOUSING CONDITIONS
EDUCATION
ETHNICITY
SEX
RACE
APPEARANCE
CITIZENSHIP
MENTAL HEALTH
RELIGION
SEXUAL ORIENTATION
GENERATION
HOBBIES & INTERESTS
LIFE EXPERIENCE
ABILITY

LESSON PLAN ASSESSMENT GUIDES

Educators all have moments when we seek existing lesson plans to use in our classrooms. When using existing lessons, it is still important to assess the quality of what we are bringing into our learning space. Tables 3.5 and 3.6 can serve as guides to ensure that you are selecting well-written, credible, and inclusive material for your lessons. These tables offer checklists to help you assess existing lesson plans (Table 3.5) and the reading material you will use (Table 3.6).

When choosing texts for the classroom, we must approach the task with the same careful consideration we would give the lesson itself. Texts should be relevant, high quality, and diverse, and they should contain depth and the potential for students to connect with the material. The goal is to increase literacy skills and create a lifelong love of reading and interacting with texts across all genres. See Table 3.6 for a checklist to help you assess and select texts for your classroom and lesson use.

In addition to Table 3.6, please see APALA's (Asian/Pacific American Librarians Association) book rubric for additional guidance regarding how to ensure that othering is avoided: "Storylines should be evaluated for othering characteristics, such as an overemphasis on the 5 Fs—food, festivals, folklore, famous people, fashion—or an overemphasis on immigration, looking different, etc." (Breslin et al., 2021).

In addition to evaluating the reading material utilized in lessons, also consider the author and/or illustrator of the texts (see Table 3.7).

Table 3.5. Considerations When Planning Lessons

Considerations	Yes	No	Notes and Reflections
Might your positionality inform ideas about the content of the lesson? How?			
Does the lesson help work toward dismantling stereotypes, tropes, myths, or misinformation? How?			
Does the lesson reflect that you engaged with your own unlearning? Have you considered what else you might need to examine or research?			
Does the lesson allow students to connect, share stories, and discuss?			
Does the lesson center the histories, stories, or experiences of traditionally marginalized persons or communities?			
Is there a voice or perspective that might be missing from the lesson? Whose?			
Have you considered how this lesson could be more culturally and community responsive or immersive?			
Does the lesson support inquiry-based learning?			
Are there multiple ways for students to demonstrate understanding of the content and objectives?			
Does the lesson allow students to make connections to self and the world?			
Are there gaps you want to fill in related to your own knowledge about the lesson? What are they?			

Table 3.6. Considerations When Choosing Texts/Reading Material Utilized in Lessons

Considerations	Yes	No	Notes and Reflections
Have you considered biases or misinformation that may exist in the text?			
What supplemental texts or articles can you include to offer a perspective from an additional culture/community/ethnicity?			
Have you considered what aspects of history the author may have overlooked?			
Have you considered which voices are present and which are not?			
Have you considered the author's own lived experience and background?			
Have you verified the author's sources and research?			
Does the text contain content that will allow students to discuss, analyze, and experience inquiry-based learning? Consider how.			
Does the text support perspective-taking?			
Does the text allow students to make text–self and text–world connections?			
Does the text center stories and histories not often illuminated?			
Are there aspects of the plot, character development, and so on that might hinder cultural responsiveness?			
Are aspects of the text diverse and inclusive (e.g., characters, themes, etc.)?			
Does the text offer opportunities for reflection and discussion?			
Does the text help dismantle stereotypes, tropes, and myths that negatively impact people and/or communities? How?			

(*continued*)

Table 3.6. Considerations When Choosing Texts/Reading Material Utilized in Lessons (*continued*)

Considerations	Yes	No	Notes and Reflections
Have you considered your own unlearning that needs to occur regarding the text(s) being used?			
Does the text lend itself to varied learning opportunities and modalities?			
Have you considered the roles of agency and power in the text and what might need to be considered related to this?			
What gaps do you want to fill in related to your own knowledge about the text?			
Does the text encourage analytical thinking and analysis?			
Are settings, themes, and characters in the text inclusive, diverse, and accurately represented?			
Does the text rely on accurate historical information?			
How can you use the un/HUSH framework to include materials that increase cultural competency?			

Table 3.7. Considerations for Authors/Illustrators of Texts Utilized in Lessons

Considerations	Yes	No	Notes and Reflections
Does the author or illustrator demonstrate cultural competence? How?			
Are students being asked to discuss, investigate, and make connections that allow them to consider the author's or illustrator's areas of possible bias?			
Can you provide supplemental texts or materials to demonstrate additional perspectives or voices? What are they?			
Have you ensured that the author's or illustrator's perspective is not primarily patriarchal or Eurocentric?			

(*continued*)

Considerations	Yes	No	Notes and Reflections
Have you considered the author's or illustrator's own lived experiences and background? What do you know about the author or illustrator that might be important?			
Does the author or illustrator demonstrate their research and sources? Did you take the time to look at their sources?			

Table 3.8 poses questions to consider when evaluating student learning activities that demonstrate understanding of objectives or standards.

Finally, I ask that you think about what worthwhile resources consider (see Figure 3.4 on the next page).

PRESERVICE TEACHER GUIDANCE

As an educator, you will have the task of discerning credible and worthwhile resources from the less effective ones. You may wonder where to start and how to go about doing this. Trial and error is a good way to assess whether a resource works for your classroom needs. Another component to consider is the research or data tied to a resource. Make certain that your resources come from credible expertise. Also ensure that you offer students their own opportunity to research, and share your knowledge with them about what credible and relevant research looks like. Classroom resources should support your learning goals, be multimodal, and be accessible to students and parents. If you provide resources to students, share some of those with members of the student's support system so that they also are a part of the learning process.

Table 3.8. Considerations for Activities That Demonstrate Understanding of Objectives/Standards

Considerations	Yes	No	Notes and Reflections
Does the activity build long-term skills and knowledge? Real-world learning? How?			
Are there multiple and varied ways for students to demonstrate understanding of the content or objectives?			
Does the lesson support critical thinking and inquiry-based learning? How?			
Are students being asked to analyze, discuss, investigate, and make connections?			
Does the lesson contribute to students being civically aware or engaged? How?			
Does the lesson and/or activity illuminate and elevate marginalized histories and stories? How?			

Figure 3.4. What Do Worthwhile Resources Consider?

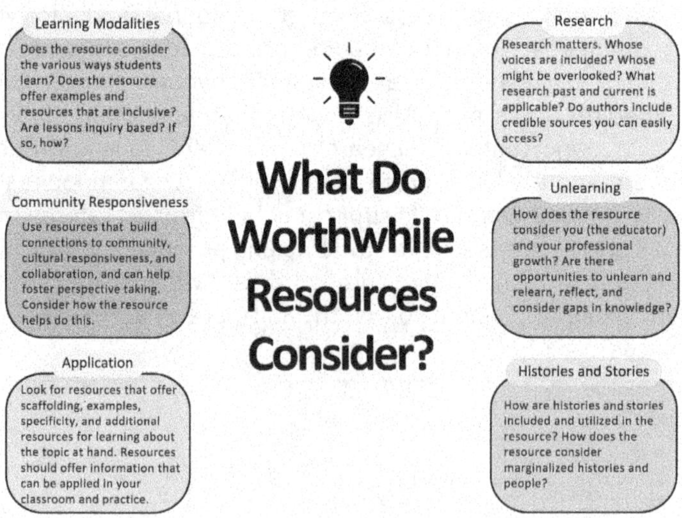

PAUSE AND REFLECT

- What resource discussed in this chapter will you commit to trying or consistently using? How will it enhance or support your classroom or teaching craft?
- Think of an existing lesson that could be revised and improved by using the framework or any of the resources provided in this chapter. Make a list of the aspects of the lesson you want to improve upon.
- Choose one topic from among the 30-day challenge topics (see Appendix D, Figure D.1) to learn about, and then journal your reflections.
- Discover a credible website with resources, explore it, and discover something new to bring to your classroom.
- In the face of resistance, how will you work to help dismantle the fears among fellow educators related to teaching marginalized stories and histories in the classroom?
- Find one text often utilized in your classroom, and then use the text evaluation checklist (Table 3.6) to practice using this resource and evaluate whether the text is culturally relevant.
- Review the sample lesson plans from Appendix C. Which one would benefit your classroom? Can you modify any of the examples to support your classroom's learning goals or objectives?
- Do you have questions about or need support with any of the resources offered in this chapter? Reach out to me via my website at https://www.marleebunch.com to connect.

CHAPTER 4

Utilizing the Arts to Enhance Learning

Utiliser les arts pour améliorer l'apprentissage (French)

> We must recognize and nurture the creative parts of each other without always understanding what will be created.
>
> —Audre Lorde

When I think about art, I think about culture, diversity, and the nuances and beauty of underrepresented stories. I do not believe you can have culturally and community responsive teaching and immersion without the arts present. Historically, art has been used throughout Black and Brown communities as a means of finding joy, making sense of the world, and self-expression. The sorrow songs of the cotton fields would evolve into the blues. Call and response would influence gospel music and poetry. Phillis Wheatly Peters would craft poems as an enslaved woman that would lead to the legacies of poets who followed. The arts are synonymous with allowing people to demonstrate expressions of their culture, this being particularly important when history and systems denied marginalized people such expression.

Although the arts are often left out of mainstream curricula, they are an integral part of intellectualism and learning (Alridge et al., 2021). Therefore, culturally responsive teaching and art are both necessary for allowing students the opportunity to explore their own cultures and those of others and to understand the vastness of their abilities. Art educators argue that arts activities encouraging students to actively explore racial, ethnic, or cultural identities and issues will assist meaningful intercultural learning (Delacruz et al., 2009). Art can illuminate that which might have been previously overlooked (Eisner, 2002). The un/HUSH framework connects directly to the arts, as it is about unearthing beauty and discovering ways to connect us to others, ourselves, and community. While all art is worthwhile, in this chapter I will focus on poetry, creative writing, and visual art, as those are what I have utilized extensively throughout my teaching.

THE POWER OF POETRY

Poetry is important and powerful, especially when used in the classroom. As an English teacher, I have used poetry to connect students to content, build relationships, and make learning relevant. I first witnessed the power of poetry as I was trying to meet the needs of a class filled with students who had various learning needs and a myriad of hurdles in their home lives. Despite students' various academic needs, what connected them to one another was the fact that they were all navigating real-world issues. Poetry provided a space to process, think through, and make sense of the upheaval and uncertainty they were facing. They wrote about losing loved ones and about issues with family, divorce, and first love. Writing creatively instilled the desire to write outside of the classroom and made writing and reading feel accessible. Writing gave them the space to feel their emotions in their raw form, and so writing became a place of respite. Most importantly, it allowed students to see they were not alone, and as they began to share their writing with one another, they understood that telling their story was powerful.

Poetry is an ideal way to implement the use of stories in your classroom while also building literacy skills and creative thinking. Resources such as *Rose, Where Did You Get That Red?* by Kenneth Koch (1973/1990) or *The Teachers & Writers Handbook of Poetic Forms* by Ron Padgett (2007) are great additions to help navigate incorporating poetry into the classroom. Victoria Chang's (2021) book *Dear Memory* shares this insight: "when you shared poems with me, you were filling the space between us with language" (p. 45). This is a beautiful way to think about the power of poetry. The list of poetic forms in Appendix F is a great place to start when bringing poetry into the classroom.

Diverse Voices: Poetry Representing a Multitude of Voices

"Reading poetry from diverse cultures invites students to experience the world from another's perspective, to take abstract concepts and make them specific, particular, and human" (Lasky et al., 2013, p. 200). Poetry removes the borders of standardized language; it is itself a diverse making of writing and thoughts as it blends different forms of writing and systems of language. Using diverse texts and a range of poetry in the classroom is a way to usher in the voices and perspectives of other cultures and people, which can increase engagement with classroom activities.

The diversity of poetry allows students to build empathy and better understand their identity, and it helps build a multicultural and global perspective. Imagine exposing students to Phillis Wheatly's poems and then showing them the work of Maya Angelou, Amanda Gorman, Ashley Jones, Evie Shockley, or Claudia Rankine—tracing the legacy of Black women. These women offer various perspectives, illustrating that individuals from the same culture are not a monolith and that experiences vary.

Additionally, poetry can help celebrate cultures and intersectionality. For example, having students read a poem by Victoria Chang in conjunction with poems by Terrance Hayes, Ariana Benson, or Nate Marshall would offer a rich tapestry of experiences to pair with a lesson, opening doors for meaningful conversations and text–self connections. Activities such as inviting students to explore languages other than their own or writing a poem in their native language build a natural sense of inclusion and appreciation. Poetry helps us remember what it is to be human.

Poetry of Witness Activity

Poetry of witness is an example of how poetry can embody histories, oral histories, global awareness, and stories—all of which work well with the un/HUSH framework. The term was initially coined by poet Carolyn Forché (1993) in her introduction to *Against Forgetting: Twentieth-Century Poetry of Witness*. Forché defines poetry of witness as bearing witness to historical events and "inhabiting the social sphere, a space between the personal and political" (p. 31). She says that these poems are "both an event and the trace of an event" (p. 33). They are poems that exemplify experiences and histories and build the sentiment that bearing witness to our own lives and those of others matters.

Take, for example, Forché's poem "The Colonel," which was written based on her experiences in El Salvador while war was occurring in the country during the 1970s. The poem reflects on the author's experience as she has dinner with a colonel who recounts stories. This type of poetry blends journalism, creative writing, and history, offering students insights into a variety of writing styles and histories. In an advanced or postsecondary class, students could discuss the historical aspect of the poem and its content using the un/HUSH framework. Poetry of witness shows students that writing can be an act of tracing history.

Ask students to read the following lines: "The parrot said hello on the terrace. The colonel told it to shut up and pushed himself from the table. My friend said to me with his eyes: say nothing."

- What (H) Histories are embedded here? What context can we discover by these lines alone?
- (U) Unlearning would involve the educator researching in advance the historical aspects of the poem and considering how to present this information and history to students.
- What (S) Stories do we hear in these lines? What do they tell us?
- What (H) Healing might students imagine through discussing the poem, sharing their interpretations, and analyzing the historical aspects of the text?

Table 4.1 provides some ideas for incorporating poetry into the classroom.

Input From Poets on Teaching Poetry

Poetry can, admittedly, be intimidating and daunting, but it also allows us to break down barriers and boundaries, which allows new ways of thinking to emerge. Later in this chapter, I share 10 poems with you that I chose because they connect to my research and to the themes of this book; they elicit thoughts and images of ancestry, education, strong women, history, and stories. These poems are for your enjoyment and personal use in the classroom. They are intended to help us become more open to language and stories outside of ourselves, as they move us out of our comfort zone and ask us to experiment with language, content, and ideas. I share them with you as examples of the powerful ways in which poetry can offer us a different vantage point and space to imagine.

You are not alone if you are wondering where to start with poetry. Fifteen years ago, I knew I wanted to use poetry more often in the classroom, but I did not want to do so haphazardly, and I knew

Table 4.1. Poetry in the Classroom

Activity	Example
Poetry competitions or poetry readings are ways to build excitement about poetry. You can also sponsor a poetry/creative writing club.	Host a schoolwide poetry reading and ask students to submit poems in advance so you can manage allotted time.
Offer extra credit to students if they go to a local poetry reading or poetry event.	Most cities offer poetry events. Additionally, there are virtual poetry events that students can access.
Create a poetry book in your classroom and fill it with poems your students write. Publish one copy through a print-on-demand online platform.	Create an end-of-year poetry collection, self-publish it, and print through an online print-on-demand site.
Use video poems to teach literary skills and help students appreciate the power of imagery and the imagination. Video poems are poems in video form; they often use art, cinema, adaptations, or recitations.	Examples of video poems are available online. Two possible sources are the Continental Review (https://www.thecontinentalreview.com) and the Windfall Room (https://www.windfallroom.com). Students can watch existing video poems or create their own.
Invite a poet to visit your classroom to speak about poetry or watch a video where poets speak about their craft.	Invite a poet to visit in person or virtually (offer a stipend to support the artist). If that is not an option, students can view interviews with poets online or in the PBS series *Poetry in America* (https://www.poetryinamerica.org).
Collaborate with art or music teachers in your building to find creative ways to incorporate poetry with other art forms.	Students can create a poem inspired by art, music, and so forth. This could be a collaborative endeavor with an art or music class.

I had much to learn. I emailed several published poets (many of whom also teach poetry) and asked them for advice and guidance. Here are the questions I asked and some of their responses. I hope these exchanges help you feel more confident and prepared in taking the leap toward using poetry in your own learning space.

What words of advice would you offer a teacher attempting to teach poetry or creative writing?

- "Teach lots of different kinds of poetry so that students don't assume that poetry is a single thing."—Joshua Marie Wilkinson
- "Students are often stalled by thoughts like 'I don't know what to write about' or 'I don't know what to say.' Encouraging students that writing is a process of discovery and it's ok to write about things you don't know about or want to know about."—Michelle Taransky
- "Show poetry, don't explain it. Let it seep in."—Tom Beckett
- "Teachers should help students explore how an interest in poetry can be pursued in the larger context of one's life. How poetry enlightens the imagination and in doing so provides a sense of awe! Poetry teaches us different systems of logic."—Emily Pettit
- "Teachers should make students aware of phanopoeia, melopoeia, and logopoeia (sight in poetry, sound in poetry, and the magic of naming words themselves). Encourage students to make what they write visible in the mind. Don't underestimate the ability of students. Challenge them at the level you would like to be challenged."—Paul Hoover
- "Help students understand negative capability (the ability to be comfortable within uncertainty and apparent contradiction) by framing it as a mind-state with which they are familiar in non-poetic contexts. Like movies, relationships, sports, work, etc. Try to draw a line between the unique ability of poetry to destabilize expectation, and the way that life in more familiar contexts destabilizes our expectations all the time, to expand meaning."—Mark Leidner

What misconceptions about poetry exist?

- "That a poem is about some secret thing designed to elude the reader. A poem is just an 'act of the mind at work' (paraphrasing poet Wallace Stevens). It's a record, a process, a thinking, an exchange, a document, a kind of thinking-inaction, tinkering with the unknown."—Joshua Marie Wilkinson
- "That poems are puzzles to be solved is one great misconception. Do not treat poems like puzzles."—Emily Pettit

- "The idea that poems are riddles and that there is one answer to what a poem *means* rather than believing that a poem is a body unto itself, some of which is perfectly mysterious and some of which is not. Also, teachers don't have to write poetry to read poetry or teach it. One does not have to be a master of something to appreciate it." —Camille Dungy
- "Poetry is often not viewed as enjoyable. Poetry is enjoyable. It can be abstract like music and art, and also be precise like a photo. It doesn't need to teach a 'lesson.'"—Maxine Chernoff

Teachers and students sometimes say, "I don't get it." Teachers then teach poems with the idea of "cracking the code." How can we avoid that approach?

- "Experimenting! Instead of focusing on the finished product like we do in critical writing, focus and celebrate moments when we are lost, we are flailing, and acknowledge that poems behave like life. Just like we don't always know the answer to a question, our poems can be problems, or incomplete sentences, or disasters. Think of writing as a science experiment where we're not working towards a conclusion, but instead, explosions and overturned hypothesis are ok, and there's no need to know the plan.

  "Also, don't ask what the poem is 'really' doing. Instead, start loving poems. Talk about what the poems are doing. Poems are not metaphors. Poems use metaphors. I like how anaphora is working here. This simile creates in me a sense of. . . . Talk about the color orange. Talk about the many things that are orange. Let poems move your mind to many things and places. Let it be messy. Let it make little sense. Let logic look like a feeling."—Emily Pettit
- "Does real value come from what is instantly knowable? What happened to struggling with questions? Make a question interesting enough and people will rise to the occasion. Immerse students in as much variety as possible and better things will happen. Not everyone can get everything."—Tom Beckett
- "Start with what students do recognize (well, there's a lot of . . . insects or drama or fragmentation, etc.) and work from there with what you notice. Students and teachers

have to trust what they notice in the poem and start to develop their own connections about how the poem works, how it presents a picture of the world to us.

"Also, avoid at every step thinking about what the poet 'intended.' It's not that they intended nothing, but the job of the reader is not to guess what may have been on the poet's mind, but instead to think *how* the language presents the world to us. I always ask: what kind of world is here?"—Joshua Marie Wilkinson

- "Developing a tolerance for confusion and the unknown is important, and poetry requires us to give up some level of control over the outcome. It's okay to refrain from analysis right away. It's okay to take what we thought we knew and suspend judgment to learn something different."—Jordan Stempleman

Are there any exercises or lessons you can share that you have found to be successful when teaching poetry to students?

- "Open each class for one week with a poem of your selection being read out loud by a student or by you. Read it at the same time each day, like a ceremony. Sometimes it's helpful to hear it read again, in someone else's voice. One can learn a lot about poetry simply by hearing it." —Paul Hoover
- "Ask students to write one-paragraph stories that intentionally make no sense—to see what unintentional forms of sense emerge. Exquisite corpse exercises [see explanation in Table 4.2] are effective first-day exercises to demonstrate how funny, sad, or true 'negative capability' [the ability to be comfortable within uncertainty and apparent contradiction] can be in a poem. Encouraging students to share their writing aloud is another way to facilitate their investment in what they write."—Mark Leidner

In *Rose, Where Did You Get That Red?* Kenneth Koch (1973/1990) shares this advice: "To help children write well and enjoy it, perhaps the most important thing to do, I found, is to be positive about everything" (p. xlvi). Table 4.2 shares some varied and accessible poetry activities that are enjoyable and realistic to implement, and that offer tangible ways to introduce poems and build a classroom that appreciates poetry.

Table 4.2. Accessible Poetry Activities and Exercises

Activities and Exercises	Guiding Instructions	Grade Level
Exquisite Corpse exercise	1. Take a piece of paper and ask the first student to write a sentence, folding over the paper to conceal what was written. 2. The paper then is passed to the next student and the next, each time concealing the newly written line. Repeat until all students have written a line.	K–12
Choose one poem and read it every day for a week at the start of class. Use any poem of your choice or choose from the 10 poems included in this chapter.	Read the poem out loud or make a copy of the poem so students can read it individually. Students can also take turns having a day to read the poem to the class.	K–12
Erasure poetry or blackout poetry exercise	1. Remove words or lines from an existing document or poem by crossing out or blacking out unwanted text. 2. The remaining text or source material creates a new poem.	6–12
Introduce one new poetic form each week and let students practice with the various forms. *Rose, Where Did You Get That Red?* or *Making Your Own Days* by Kenneth Koch or *The Teachers & Writers Handbook of Poetic Forms* by Ron Padgett are helpful resources.	See Appendix F for explanations of various poetic forms.	K–12
Epistolary/epistle poem exercise	Students can read an example of an epistle poem and then write their own. An epistle is a poem written in the form of a letter. See "6.3.96–6.4.96" by June Jordan or "Theme for English B" by Langston Hughes as examples.	6–12

(*continued*)

Table 4.2. Accessible Poetry Activities and Exercises (*continued*)

Activities and Exercises	Guiding Instructions	Grade Level
Six-word memoir exercise. Visit https://www.sixwordmemoirs.com where students can see examples and submit their own six-word memoirs.	Six-word memoirs sum up a moment in one's life in six words. Writer Ernest Hemingway's was "for sale, baby shoes never worn."	5–12
Read a poem out loud and ask students to draw the images they visualize in the poem.	Try reading "Jabberwocky" by Lewis Carroll out loud. Ask younger students to draw what they think the Jabberwock looks like. Or read a Claudia Rankine poem to older students and ask them to illustrate the scene and images the poem evokes.	K–12
Ekphrastic poetry exercise (poems written about art or an image)	Display an image (art image, current event image, etc.) for the class to view. Ask students to write a short ekphrastic poem in response to the image.	6–12
Show a video of a poet reading a poem. *The Poem I Wish I Had Read* (a series featured by Smith College) is a great place to start.	Ask students to write a bell work response or journal entry that includes their thoughts and reactions to the poem.	6–12
Ask students to create a cento poem. A traditional cento has 100 lines and is a "patchwork" poem created by using lines from other poets. You can do a modified cento if time is limited (e.g., 50 lines). This form is a way to introduce research, as it requires reviewing the work of various poets to find lines to use. It is also a way to introduce how to carefully credit other writers' work, and what plagiarism entails and does not entail.	Students can begin researching different poets and poems online. They write down any lines they like, compiling lines until they reach 100. Students then reorder the lines to create a new poem and credit each poet for the lines they use (see Figure 4.1; the poets used are numbered and cited, giving credit to each one).	6–12

Figure 4.1. Student Example of Modified Cento Poem (the Second Image Shows the Poets Used in the Cento)

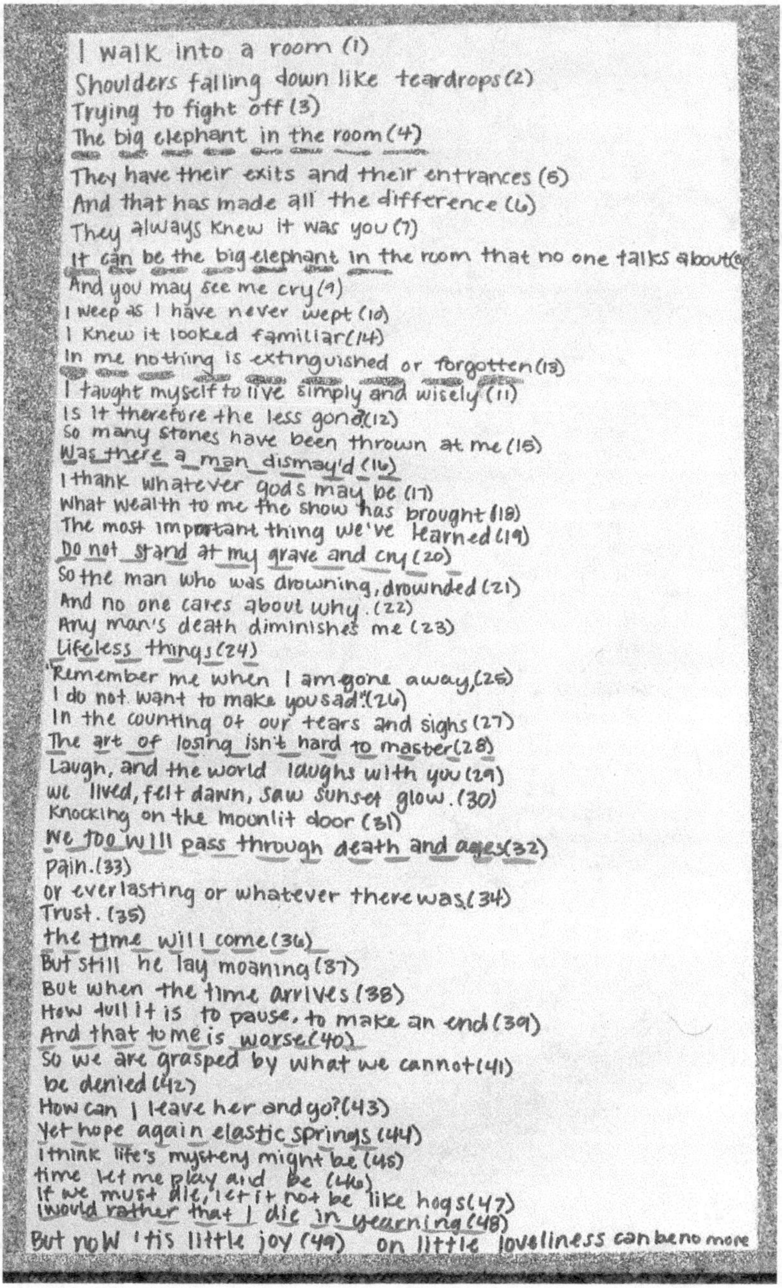

I walk into a room (1)
Shoulders falling down like teardrops (2)
Trying to fight off (3)
The big elephant in the room (4)
They have their exits and their entrances (5)
And that has made all the difference (6)
They always knew it was you (7)
It can be the big elephant in the room that no one talks about(8)
And you may see me cry (9)
I weep as I have never wept (10)
I knew it looked familiar (14)
In me nothing is extinguished or forgotten (13)
I taught myself to live simply and wisely (11)
Is it therefore the less gone (12)
So many stones have been thrown at me (15)
Was there a man dismay'd (16)
I thank whatever gods may be (17)
What wealth to me the show has brought (18)
The most important thing we've learned (19)
Do not stand at my grave and cry (20)
So the man who was drowning, drownded (21)
And no one cares about why. (22)
Any man's death diminishes me (23)
Lifeless things (24)
"Remember me when I am gone away, (25)
I do not want to make you sad." (26)
In the counting of our tears and sighs (27)
The art of losing isn't hard to master (28)
Laugh, and the world laughs with you (29)
We lived, felt dawn, saw sunset glow. (30)
Knocking on the moonlit door (31)
We too will pass through death and ages (32)
pain. (33)
or everlasting or whatever there was (34)
Trust. (35)
the time will come (36)
But still he lay moaning (37)
But when the time arrives (38)
How dull it is to pause, to make an end (39)
And that to me is worse (40)
So we are grasped by what we cannot (41)
be denied (42)
How can I leave her and go? (43)
Yet hope again elastic springs (44)
I think life's mystery might be (45)
time let me play and be (46)
If we must die, let it not be like hogs (47)
I would rather that I die in yearning (48)
But now 'tis little joy (49) on little loveliness can be no more

Figure 4.1. Student Example of Modified Cento Poem (the Second Image Shows the Poets Used in the Cento) (*continued*)

1. Maya Angelou "Phenomenal Woman"
2. Maya Angelou "Still I Rise"
3. Charles Bukowski "And The Moon And The Stars And The World"
4. Drake J. Eszes "The Elephant in the Room"
5. Sylvia Plath "Daddy"
6. Robert Frost "The Road Not Taken"
7. William Shakespeare "All The World's A Stage"
8. Emily Pettit "How To Hide an Elephant"
9. Langston Hughes "Life Is Fine"
10. Christina Rossetti "A Daughter of Eve"
11. Anna Akhmatova "I Taught Myself To Live Simply
12. Edgar Allen Poe "A Dream Within A Dream"
13. Pablo Neruda "If You Forget Me"
14. Shel Silverstein "Messy Room"
15. Anna Akhmatova "White Flock"
16. Lord Alfred Tennyson "The Charge of the Light Brigade"87
17. William Ernest Henley "Invictus: The Unconquerable"
18. William Wordsworth "Daffodils"
19. Roald Dahl "Television"
20. Mary Frye "Do Not Stand at My Grave and Weep"
21. Spike Milligan "Have a Nice Day"
22. Tupak Shakur "I Cry"
23. John Donne "No Man is an Island"
24. Percy Bysshe Shelley
25. Christina Georgina Rosetti "Remember"
26. Alexander Sereyevich Pushkin "I Loved You"
27. Paul Laurence Dunbar "We Wear the Mask"
28. Elizabeth Bishop "One Art"
29. Ella Wheeler Wilcox "Solitude"
30. John McCrae "In Flandus Field"
31. Walter De La Mare "The Listeners"
32. Sara Teasdale "I Thought of You"
33. Mathew Arnold "Dover Beach"
34. Ted Hughes "Lovesong"
35. Rabindranath Tagore "Where the Mind is Without Fear"
36. Derek Walcott "Love after Love"
37. Stevie Smith "Not Waving but Moaning"
38. Henry David Thoreau "Friendship"
39. Alfred Lord Tennyson "Ulysses"
40. Dorothy Parker "A Very Short Song"
41. Rainer Maria Rilke "A Walk"
42. John Masefield "Sea Fever"
43. Rabindranath Tagore "Clouds and Waves"

POEMS TO USE IN THE CLASSROOM

Reading and writing poetry helps students explore the interconnectedness of people and places and avoid prescriptive thinking and the rush toward certainty. Additionally, "they can form deeper connections to other people through our most basic and important human invention: language" (Lasky et al., 2013, p. 199). The following pages include a few of my favorite poems by beloved poets. I thank them all for their important contributions of words and beauty. I have seen the underinclusion of poetry and creativity in curriculum, and I encourage you to explore ways to bring creative writing and art into your spaces, as it helps preserve stories and ideas that might otherwise be underappreciated. Table 4.3 offers a snapshot of the forthcoming poems and helps you consider how you will utilize them in your learning space. As you are preplanning and planning lessons and activities, use Table 4.3 as a guide to determine how the poems might fit into lessons or units, and how they might enhance other texts. The table offers information about literary devices the poems can illuminate, questions for students to consider when experiencing the poem(s), and how each poem connects to the un/HUSH framework. Additionally, you will find a few poetry exercises to use in the classroom that correlate with some of the featured poems.

Poetry is beautiful and hard. There are no right answers or code to crack, and there is no pressure to have all the answers. Good educators say, "I don't know everything about this poem, but I like this line because. . . ." Like music, sometimes you just have to *feel* the poem. Do not worry if students' answers or interpretations vary—they should. Encourage students to enjoy poetry, to feel, to imagine.

As you find ways to incorporate these poems, consider inviting students to use the following questions as a starting place as they begin determining their own meanings of poems:

1. What images can you visualize in the poem?
2. Is there something you like about the poem? What is it?
3. Find a line of the poem that resonates with you.
4. How does this poem connect to other texts, history, your life, the world?
5. This poem creates in me a sense of . . .

Table 4.3. Tools for Using the Poems Included

Poem Title and Poet	Connection to un/ HUSH Framework	Literary Device(s)	Question(s) to Consider
"good night women (or, defying the carcinogenic pen)" by Evie Shockley	(S) Stories- This poem uses fragments of history to help bring together stories of women.	Imagery, metaphor (e.g., "they are like stars")	What images can you visualize in the poem?
"African American Literature I" by Ashley M. Jones (current poet laureate of Alabama)	(H) Healing- This poem connects to the framework as it conjures up feelings that students might experience in a racially mismatched classroom.	Imagery, repetition (e.g., "I exist I exist I exist . . .")	What historical information does the poem reference? What sounds or images can you hear or see?
"In Memory of Trayvon Martin" by Claudia Rankine. Hear the author read the poem: https://www.youtube.com/watch?v=0xx1dwFxAv0	(H) Healing and (H) History- This poem connects to the framework as it embodies our more recent history with racial violence.	Stanzas, line breaks, repetition (e.g., "my brothers are notorious")	How does the poem honor the idea of memory?
"Lessons" by Jordan Stempleman	(H) History and (S) Stories- This poem connects to our stories and histories that emerge in classrooms.	Line break, imagery (e.g., "the teacher's forehead empties out")	What images do you see? What does the poem evoke for you?
"Built Slowly" by Emily Pettit	(S) Stories- This poem gives us a sense of our own story growing up.	Repetition, naming (e.g., "Gertrude Gardner, Piano Bucket, Speckled Duck," etc.)	Is there something you love about the poem? How does the poem honor histories and stories?

(*continued*)

Poem Title and Poet	Connection to un/ HUSH Framework	Literary Device(s)	Question(s) to Consider
"Haint Blue" by Cole Swensen	(H) History- This poem speaks to southern ways and history, as southern porches and windows were painted the color haint blue to ward off bad spirits/ ghosts. This context can be shared when introducing the poem.	Imagery, listing (e.g., "where its edges or ashes or an eyelash")	What image can you visualize in the poem?
"Ancestors" by Mary Ruefle	(H) History and (S) Stories- This poem allows us to consider our family history and the stories within families.	Naming, imagery (e.g., "It had a soda fountain / and in the only photograph I have / he's standing behind the Moxie tap / wearing a white paper hat")	What is the poem paying the most attention to? This poem creates in me a sense of . . .
"Shhhhh, Louder" by Natasha Ria El-Scari	(H) History and (S) Stories- This poem details an experience in a classroom.	Stanzas, listing (e.g., "able to hear bees make words / and birds gossip about wasps / and hear worms play drums")	This poem creates in me a sense of . . . What is something you love about the poem?
"The Lynch Family Blues (after 'Lynch Family' by Joseph Hirsch, 1946)" by Glenn North. Hear the author read the poem: https://www.youtube.com/watch?v=Q86ggAXvr2U	(H) History- This poem connects to the history of racial violence in our country.	Imagery, repetition (e.g., the word "swingin")	How does this poem connect to other texts, history, your life, the world? What is the poem paying the most attention to?

(*continued*)

Table 4.3. Tools for Using the Poems Included *(continued)*

Poem Title and Poet	Connection to un/ HUSH Framework	Literary Device(s)	Question(s) to Consider
"America Are We Safe, Were We Ever" by Stanley Banks	(H) History- This poem encourages us to consider history and events.	Imagery, stanzas (e.g., "will a jail on every corner be enough?")	What image can you visualize in the poem?

Readers can also access the QR code material on the Teachers College Press website at https://teachers-college-press.myshopify.com/products/the-magnitude-of-us_9780807769881. The materials appear at the bottom of the web page.

Evie Shockley[1]

good night women
(or, defying the carcinogenic pen)

they are : (like stars)

rising

always brightly there behind our blindness,
pricking through the dark tent
with a fine, white rage
that burns garbage to ashes,
that fires truth to ceramic strength.

shining

beaconing us to a north we bring along
in our pockets, constellating,
andromedas fighting their own monsters,
dipping into history and wisdom,
filling to overflowing the big and little gourds.

falling

ripping hot and fierce down the night sky
till they are out of our pining sight,
too quickly, more frequently than we can bear,
their incandescent metal, incinerating, is
the occasion and inverse of wish.

—*in memory of audre lorde (1934–92) / toni cade bambara (1939–95) / sherley anne williams (1944–99) / barbara christian (1943–2000) / claudia tate (1947–2002) / june jordan (1936–2002) / nellie mckay (cir. 1933–2006)*

African American Literature I

By Ashley M. Jones[2]
for VWS

she's crazy / they said / *she's so crazy and you don't learn anything*
richard wright alice walker frantz fanon ralph ellison—nothings in disguise as somethings
look at her hair / look how it sticks out / look how she dresses / look look look
what did I see but myself in her? fro picked out and loud, fabrics draped like regal rags
she's too old to teach us / she's senile / she doesn't know what she's doing
in this world, even the phd doesn't equal proficiency—black modifies scholar
why do we even have to take this class? / I'd rather take shakespeare / milton / someone important
I exist I exist I exist I exist even though the universe says *no* in iambic pentameter
I said:
I said:
finally, I said: I am learning / she is brilliant / just learn, stop resisting / these books these stories are   mine
you only get A's because you're black / you only get A's because you're black
in this world, even an honors designation doesn't equal proficiency / black modifies student
sometimes   even   I   doubted   you
who was I to say you were wrong, who were any of us?

didn't we see that the gleam in your eye was not eccentricity, senility, but the very last drop /

of your hope?

In Memory of Trayvon Martin

By Claudia Rankine

My brothers are notorious. They have not been to prison. They have been imprisoned. The prison is not a place you enter. It is no place. My brothers are notorious. They do regular things, like wait. On my birthday they say my name. They will never forget that we are named. What is that memory?

The days of our childhood together were steep steps into a collapsing mind. It looked like we rescued ourselves, were rescued. Then there are these days, each day of our adult lives. They will never forget our way through, these brothers, each brother, my brother, dear brother, my dearest brothers, dear heart—

Your hearts are broken. This is not a secret though there are secrets. And as yet I do not understand how my own sorrow has turned into my brothers' hearts. The hearts of my brothers are broken. If I knew another way to be, I would call up a brother, I would hear myself saying, my brother, dear brother, my dearest brothers, dear heart—

On a tip of a tongue one note following another is another path, another dawn where the pink sky is the bloodshot of struck, of sleepless, of sorry, of senseless, shush. Those years of and before me and my brothers, the years of passage, plantation, migration, of Jim Crow segregation, of poverty, inner cities, profiling of one in three, two jobs, boy, hey boy, each a felony, accumulate into the hours inside our lives where we are all caught hanging, the rope inside us, the tree inside us, its roots our limbs, a throat sliced through and when we open our mouth to speak, blossoms, o blossoms, no place coming out, brother, dear brother, that kind of blue. The sky is the silence of brothers all the days leading up to my call.

If I called I'd say good-bye before I broke the good-bye. I say good-bye before anyone can hang up. Don't hang up. My brother hangs up though he is there. I keep talking. The talk keeps him there. The sky is blue, kind of blue. The day is hot. Is it cold? Are you cold? It does get cool. Is it cool? Are you cool?

My brother is completed by sky. The sky is his silence. Eventually, he says, it is raining. It is raining down. It was raining. It stopped raining. It is raining down. He won't hang up. He's there, he's there but he's hung up though he is there. Good-bye, I say. I break the good-bye. I say good-bye before anyone can hang up, don't hang up. Wait with me. Wait with me though the waiting might be the call of good-byes.

Lessons

By Jordan Stempleman

In one version of a country's history
the teacher's forehead empties out
as fog into owned open air.
But in another version
mothers are running their fingers across this
and that
the hollowed arcades from before we met
and after we eat
what we watch out for
and what could never be enough.
The cold quail.
The sparks that turn down bit by bit.
Wish now for all that can't consider be stirred.
For all that won't consider be stirred.
In all the strangers' faces
until there's the seen and the unseen.
And in all these names
that we memorize and replace
let them return to sounds that see again.
The once alien
decked out in the approximate togetherness
gone alike
in the wearing away.

Built Slowly

By Emily Pettit

Gertrude Gardner at eight received a new nickname. Piano Bucket. At seven she was known as Speckled Duck. At six as Interrogation Spiral. At five she was known as Open Field. At four she was known as the Tiny Sea. At three she was known as the Ungrounded Spirit. At two she was known as Bunny. At one she was known as BooBoo. In the womb she was known as Bird's Nest. She was being built slowly to house herself.

Haint Blue[3]

By Cole Swensen

On the frame around the porch where its edges or ashes or an eyelash
of feathering porchlight quietly annihilates darkness all throughout Georgia
the frames are painted this particular shade because it keeps the ghosts away or
keeps them closer, curled up in the home I can't remember which one was first
to point out the robin's egg laid on the third storey windowsill on the inside
a bird born within the house of such a deep blue that we've never been able to find

Ancestors

By Mary Ruefle

The best thing that ever happened to me
was that my grandparents all died
before I was born.
I've never had a sense of who I am,
and in that regard I've been lucky.
It's only natural
I know a little about them.
One grandfather worked a steel lathe,
cut off his finger and opened a bar.
The other one went to school, became
a pharmacist and owned a marvelously
tidy drugstore. It had a soda fountain
and in the only photograph I have
he's standing behind the Moxie tap
wearing a white paper hat.
One of my grandmothers, who outlived them all,
died of either a broken heart or diabetes.
The other grandmother was sadly senile
and died peacefully in her sleep.
I have a mania for soap and cologne,
hairpins and talc, but so do many of my friends
who never had a pharmacy in their past.
With the extent of my knowledge I've done okay.
I won a cakewalk once, and another time—
at a seaside carnival—a painted plate
in the shape of Rhode Island.
I don't need a quietus to sleep.
I don't need an alarm to wake.
All dreams have tragic implications.
I have the same one every year:
in Sarajevo, a queue of men
line up to have their fezzes ironed.

Shhhhh, Louder

By Natasha Ria El-Scari

When a girl comes to the planet
able to hear bees make words
and birds gossip about wasps
and hear worms play drums
she is often told to be silent.

Honesty lubricates her lips
as she articulates
like the adults do
with the same authority
only in her small body.

Now Tasha, don't say that . . .
Now Tasha, next time tell me first before you . . .
talk about God is a woman,
about men who aren't . . .
about white people who shouldn't . . .
but there would be a grin
peeking over their teeth
and she knew then
in just a while
in just awhile
she wouldn't have to raise her hand
to speak.

The Lynch Family Blues

After *Lynch Family* by Joseph Hirsch, 1946

By Glenn North

Went out swingin last night, baby
Hope you didn't wait up for me.
Said I was swingin all night, baby
Did you stay up late for me?
I wasn't swingin in no joint, darlin
I was out on the limb of a tree.

Now I'm walkin on air, baby
Feels almost like I'm free.
My feet steady kickin the wind
Yeah, I'm close to bein free.
For the first time in my life, baby
White folks is lookin up to me.

Hear me, son, your daddy loves you
Keep hangin on to hope.
You the man of the house now
Gotta help your mama cope.
Daddy won't be coming home no more
'Cause I reached the end of my rope.

America Are We Safe, Were We Ever

By Stanley Banks

Will we ever let America
be true to her huddled masses?
Why do we glorify myths,
stereotype the least amongst us,
get outraged only by
some atrocities?
America, is a little starving,
some homelessness,
factions of racism tolerable?
Are we safe among ourselves?
Will a jail on every corner
be enough?
Can our pop musicians play
our troubles into oblivion?
Can we be truly free
if a few do away with liberties
they think unnecessary?
Will it matter in the
21st Century if the
O's in the ozone are massive,
if the planet is a
totally polluted place,
if hazardous waste makes all of us
other kinds of human beings?
Should we count on scientists
producing enough genetically
perfect human beings?
Maybe one day our lives
will be fairy tales—
the Brothers Grimm our gods,
and even then can any
of us guarantee that
the bogeyman won't visit.

The following two poetry exercises correlate with the poems "African American Literature I" by Ashley M. Jones and "Built Slowly" by Emily Pettit. The first exercise, for "African American Literature I," was created and shared by poet Emily Pettit, while the second was created by me modeling her format and creating my own exercise for "Built Slowly." Pettit's format creates an accessible way for you to replicate the exercise for various other poems. Take a moment to use the poetry exercise(s) as a blueprint to create your own activities for another poem included in this book or a poem of your choosing.

After reading the poem, ask students to work through the exercise, creating their own poem with their own words. The exercise offers an opportunity for students to experiment with the abstract and the specific, which encourages them to take chances in writing, while offering them some direction.

Writing Exercise for "African American Literature I" (created by Emily Pettit)

Write 1–2 lines about a subject of study that is important to you.
Make a list of 1–5 objects/ideas that connect to the subject of study that is important to you.
Make a list of 3–5 thinkers who are important to you.
Write 1–2 lines exploring why one of these thinkers is important to you.
Write 1–2 lines exploring why another one of these thinkers is important to you.
Write 1–2 lines about feeling doubted or feeling doubt.
Make a list of 1–3 objects or ideas that connect to the feeling of being doubted and/or not valued.
Write 1–2 questions.
Choose 3–8 of your lines to collage together a poem. Should you want to use every line you've written, do so. If lines occur to you to write outside of the instructions, write them.

Writing Exercise for "Built Slowly"

Write 1–2 lines about a nickname or several nicknames you have had.
Make a list of 1–5 memories/ideas/feelings that are connected to those nicknames.

Make a list of 3–5 nicknames you *should* have had based on your curiosities and personality.

Write 1–2 lines exploring why one of these nicknames you've chosen for yourself is important to you.

Write 1–2 lines exploring the origins of the name given to you at birth and its importance.

Write 1–2 lines about the ways in which you've grown into or out of your various nicknames.

Make a list of 1–3 objects that connect to your identity, childhood, the person you've grown to be.

Write 1–2 questions.

Choose 3–8 of your lines to collage together a poem. Should you want to use every line you've written, do so. If lines occur to you to write outside of the instructions, write them.

Poetry should be both written and heard. Please find audio readings of some of the featured poems in the QR code or at https://teachers-college-press.myshopify.com/products/the-magnitude-of-us_9780807769881.

VISUAL ART IN THE CLASSROOM

Another art form I have leaned on in my teaching is the visual arts. Painting, collage, graphic novels, and so forth have all been useful in helping students delve deeper into inquiry and learning. Visual thinking strategies (VTS), developed by Philip Yenawine and Abigail Housen (https://vtshome.org), is a teaching and discussion technique focused on building critical thinking skills through the analysis of art or images. It is an approach that encourages thinking to reach beyond first interpretations. The essential aspects of VTS are as follows:

- Educators choose a visual image—in this case, any visual art image, either historical or modern—to display for students. You can also use newspaper images, images of historical artifacts, and so forth.
- Once the image is displayed, ask students this question: "What is happening here in this image?" When students begin to respond verbally, remain neutral and repeat what you heard them say back to the class. For example, if looking at a painting of an old schoolhouse, a student

might say: "I see an old schoolhouse with kids and a teacher." You repeat back what you heard: "You said you see an old schoolhouse with kids and a teacher."

- Next, encourage deeper thinking by asking students what more they can find or see: "What else do you notice or see?"
- Lastly, you can use the question "What makes you say that?" to encourage students to share rationale and details. This encourages them to use textual/visual evidence when making an analysis.

Art journals are another good way to encourage students to use VTS strategies, and they can connect to any theme you want to have students focus on (history, identity, etc.). Consider Figure 4.2, which includes questions to help students create an art journal entry about identity. Art journals explore ideas, emotions, expressions, elements of art, and so forth, and this exploration can be done through art, poetry, and/or music. Art journals do not require strong art skills but instead utilize visual thinking to express ideas and perspectives.

Visual thinking strategies work well with the un/HUSH framework. You can connect the subject matter and content to the

Figure 4.2. Art Journal and Visual Thinking Tool

ART JOURNAL

Visual thinking strategies work well with the un/HUSH framework

Reflections

How do artists question commonly held assumptions about stereotypes, self-awareness, portraiture, and what does it means to be an artist? How can images and art help us examine ourselves, the world, and others?

Idea Gathering

As you consider and visualize your own identity, think about:

- Smells, sounds, tastes, memories.
- People and places that matter to you.
- Stories related to your family or friend group.
- Self-perception.

Images

- What do you think the person in the image is about to say? What might they be thinking?
- What does their expression or body language tell us?
- What is happening in this image? What story is being told?
- What might you infer?
- Think of an image or artwork that has powerful imagery.

Visual Thinking & un/HUSH

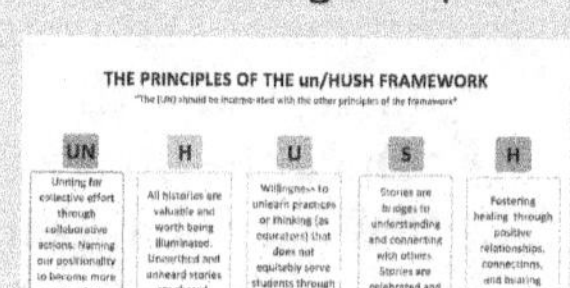

framework by asking the following questions (these questions can be used when discussing other art forms as well):

- *(H) History:* What aspects of history do we see in the image? How do you know? Is there a historical lesson apparent in the image?
- *(U) Unlearning:* What unlearning do I need to consider for myself (as the educator) before sharing this image with students? Do I have any misperceptions or bias about this image or art? Have I researched the artwork/image to adequately teach students in a culturally responsive manner?
- *(S) Stories:* What story does this image tell? How does this image connect to students' stories? Are there any untold or silenced stories in the image?
- *(H) Healing:* What does this image/artwork help us better understand about others? How can we use the artwork to connect with different perspectives/cultures/people/communities? What might the image prompt us to reflect upon about ourselves or our own life?

Visual art and poetry are easy to intertwine. Table 4.4 shares some ideas for using both together.

The Power of Images

One of the first paintings I bought was created by artist Harold Smith. I remember the first time I saw it. I was grieving the racial violence in our country and happened upon a painting of his. It was the face of a man—piercing eyes, grief-stricken face, yet it felt bold and brave. In that very moment, I felt understood in a way that didn't require words; the painting allowed me to be and to feel. That is the power of art—it can mirror and reflect our emotions and our deepest thoughts, and simultaneously amplify the beauty and pain of the world.

Table 4.5 offers a few suggestions for ways to incorporate artwork and visuals into your learning spaces.

Figure 4.3 (painting and collage) was created by a student in response to *The Perks of Being a Wallflower*. The piece examines the symbolism of the typewriter and letters in the novel. The student discussed the art in a presentation.

Table 4.4. Using Visual Art and Poetry in the Classroom

Activity	Example
Ask students to write in a journal and then add drawings, sketches, painting, collage, and so forth.	Students can add visual drawings to their journal for additional depth.
Visual maps	Students can document their own history by drawing a map of their lives.
Graphic novels and comic books	Students can analyze or summarize a text by drawing it as a graphic novel. If the class reads a required text, allow students to reimagine it in graphic novel form.
Go to a museum or tour a museum online and access their many resources for students.	Museum resources and virtual tours allow students to connect content to history and visual thinking.
Collage art	Recreate a poem using only images in collage form.
Use *New York Times* images to practice visual thinking strategies: https://www.nytimes.com/2021/07/28/learning/introduction-to-whats-going-on-in-this-picture.html. This additional website encourages students to observe the details of art: https://www.nytimes.com/interactive/2021/arts/close-read.html	Use images to engage in brief class discussions about inferences as you work together to analyze the images.

The scrapbook shown in Figure 4.4 was created by a student who also examined the themes and character of *The Perks of Being a Wallflower*. The student used each scrapbook page to analyze various elements of the text. The pages shown in Figure 4.4 examined the main character's relationships with his teacher/school and his friend group. The student shared the scrapbook in small-group discussions.

The two poetry chapbooks shown in Figure 4.5 were created by our class. The one on the left was done using a copy machine, and the one on the right shows a print-on-demand end product.

Relating the visual to the historical is important because it allows connections to occur in students' minds. As learners and generations become more dependent on visual information, ensuring

Table 4.5. Activities Using Visuals and Artwork in the Classroom

Activity	Example
Create a walking gallery or classroom museum.	Gather students' work to hang or display on the classroom wall or in the hallway, then allow students to walk the space to observe, compare/contrast, and analyze. Invite other classes to view the gallery.
Ask students to create a visual that sums up a theme/ learning objective/summary from a lesson or unit.	Visuals could include a painting, collage art, slide deck, or diagram.
Give students canvas or paper and let them paint an image that correlates with textual evidence. Making connections is an important part of learning.	Allow students to create a painting related to a theme of a text. For example, if students read Stephen Chbosky's *The Perks of Being a Wallflower*, perhaps the painting might be of the tunnel scene or the typewriter image. Students can include a written analysis of why the scene or image is relevant. (See Figure 4.3 for an example.)
If you are an ELA or history teacher, have students create yearbooks or scrapbooks of a fictional or historical character.	What would the yearbook or scrapbook of a book's character look like? If students read *The Perks of Being a Wallflower*, what would Charlie's yearbook look like? What would his scrapbook entail? (See Figure 4.4 for an example.)
Collaborate with the art teacher in your building to co-create a lesson that utilizes art.	This collaboration could be as simple as a hallway bulletin board or could involve teaching a text and coordinating with the art teacher to plan a portraiture assignment.
Students can create a memoir or introduction to themselves using photographs.	This might include a slide deck or a PechaKucha presentation (a format that uses 20 slides, one image per slide, images are displayed for 20 seconds each). See https://www.pechakucha.com for more details.
Students can make chapbooks, scrapbooks, or zines using paper and simple materials. Invite other classes, teachers, and members of administration in the building to contribute.	Making chapbooks (small booklets) or zines (self-published books) can be done through do-it-yourself methods or with print-on-demand sites. Instructions for both options are easily found online. (See Figure 4.5 for examples.)

(*continued*)

Table 4.5. Activities Using Visuals and Artwork in the Classroom (*continued*)

Activity	Example
Have students create collages.	Collage art can be made with materials such as paper, magazines, images, words, and so on. Collage art asks students to consider the connectedness between things.
Raise or request funds to invite a local artist to speak to your classroom or school. For example, does your city have a mural painting? Invite the artist who painted it to speak about art and the mural.	Engage the community by inviting local artists to share their expertise (offer artists a stipend for their time).
Make a visual journal for any of the components of the framework (histories, stories, unlearning, healing).	Students can use only images to visually document their (H) history, (U) unlearning, (S) stories that have impacted their lives, and how they envision (H) healing.

Figure 4.3. Example of Student Artwork

Figure 4.4. Example of Student Scrapbook

Figure 4.5. Examples of Poetry Chapbooks

that there is an entry point for all learning styles is essential. Visuals are also a means to elevate people and communities often overlooked, to create artifacts, and to foster cultural awareness (Davenport, 2000; Delacruz et al., 2009).

I wanted to use visuals in my own research to honor my participants' stories. I acknowledged their stories by having the images of the women who guided my study displayed on a gallery wall. I collaborated with a local artist (Kevin Hopkins) to bring these stories and histories to life. Haw Contemporary Gallery (Kansas City, Missouri) featured the exhibit, and I was able to see firsthand the

Figure 4.6. Artwork "Mother I Graduated" by Kevin Hopkins

power of images and visual representation, as well as the importance of community immersive experiences.

Figure 4.6 is an example of one of the art pieces developed for the exhibit. This collage uses images from Mississippi students who attended school between the 1950s and 1970s, my grandmothers, and the artist's mother, along with other historical photographs related to Mississippi history. This image represents the past and the present—mentors, ancestors, grandmothers, teachers. It is a symbol of community and collective strength. It is a quilting together of histories that make stories visually evident, a way to say we are here. Having students create their own version of this collage would be a powerful classroom activity. Students could create a collage that visually traces and embeds their history, ancestry, and lineage. Using this visual activity alongside the un/HUSH framework would allow students to employ all the principles of the un/HUSH framework in conjunction with activating the arts. I imagine that using the two in tandem would create a meaningful learning experience for students.

Using the arts in the classroom is a way to celebrate inclusion and diversity, build connections, create community, and work toward healing. The arts celebrate diversity, as there are past and contemporary artists representing a wide array of backgrounds that can be introduced into the classroom (Jean-Michel Basquiat, Frida

Kahlo, and Yayoi Kusama, among others). Using the arts helps build connections and community, as you can craft lessons that center stories and students and you can collaborate with fellow educators and the community to bring the arts into your learning space. The arts offer students opportunities to reflect, see themselves, and witness the experiences of others.

Research suggests four elements for inquiry for the arts. These elements offer a guide to creating optimal learning when incorporating the arts into your learning space:

1. Direct experiences
2. Observations and reflections
3. Deliberation and dialogue
4. Collaborative actions (Krug & Parker, 2009)

These four elements complement the un/HUSH framework and reiterate the value of making the arts part of regular pedagogical practice, and they offer additional support for integrating arts into curricula.

Using artwork, poetry, and visuals is an effective way to utilize the un/HUSH framework and connect students to learning content. Art and poetry give us myriad possibilities to bring diverse and rich perspectives into classrooms. Artwork and poetry also offer us the opportunity to document and acknowledge typically silenced or marginalized histories. This chapter has covered many suggestions for ways to incorporate the arts into your classroom pedagogy. Implementing art in your classroom will enrich learning and create new possibilities for expression, because somewhere inside of us, we are all creatives just waiting for an invitation to explore and think without restraint.

PRESERVICE TEACHER GUIDANCE

No matter what subject or what grade level you will be teaching, I encouage you to use art in your spaces, lessons, and practices—anything from allowing a student to bring in a visual to decorate the classroom walls, to playing music as students enter the classroom. Art helps to expand learning and build connections. Art can sometimes be intimidating, because it involves so many aspects, and we worry that we do not have the expertise to teach art. The wonderful thing about art is that there are many answers and perspectives, so the odds of getting it wrong are low. Offer it as an option for students, and let *them* guide where it goes. Art is a natural place to start your endeavors of collaborating with others. Bring in speakers and community members who are experts in a specific area, or connect with the art teacher in your building. Host a forensics or theatre show in your clasroom after school, display a virtual tour of a museum, reach out to local art galleries and museums for resources, and so on. There are endless opportunities for you and your students to explore. Let art be a reprieve, a place for enjoyment and wonder.

PAUSE AND REFLECT

- How have you used art in your classroom previously? What is one suggestion from Chapter 4 that you will try?
- What are two lessons or objectives you hope to teach all students that art would help you articulate?
- Name one poem and one visual art piece you appreciate. How can you bring them into your classroom to enhance learning?
- What elements of art help learners read between the lines to infer and excavate subtext?
- How might art help foster an appreciation for other cultures, traditions, and so forth? How might it encourage a global learning?

Listening to Our Students

Escuchando a nuestros estudiantes (Spanish)

> We are each other's harvest; we are each other's business; we are each other's magnitude and bond.
>
> —Gwendolyn Brooks

My former student Xyanne Purnell told me, "It is vital to our future that we shift our focus back to the way we learn, the way we are taught, and ultimately, the way we teach each other. We must ensure that we are equipped with the proper resources needed to not only survive but evolve through oppression, inequality, and emotional ignorance. These seeds are often planted early on, in spaces as common as a classroom. This is why it is important that we create spaces and systems that foster individuality, vulnerability, growth, and healing. . . . There is one role we all share that is undeniable and that is to be a student—to remain willing to unlearn what has been misinformed, making room to learn new methods of efficiency, conquering growth one day at a time. One lesson at a time. The lessons we are taught throughout our lives will shape the people we decide to be, the choices we make, and so much more."

Students have the power to help us realize the value of the bonds we build and the relationships we forge through teaching. As Gwendolyn Brooks says, students teach us that we are each other's business, each other's harvest (Brooks, 2005), and through listening to and watching them, I have learned to embed that thinking in my classroom culture and practice.

One of the most powerful lessons I learned early in my teaching career was to listen to my students. Their suggestions, feedback, and insights were always worthwhile, and from listening to their words, I in turn became a more intentional and effective educator. Listening to students makes all the difference and helps build equitable classrooms (Hammond, 2020).

Young people know more than they are often given credit for, and when educators offer them space that gives them autonomy, I have seen them show up in the most impressive ways. I encourage you to ask your students for feedback, consider their input, and foster their voices.

I cannot think of a better way to illustrate the power of listening and learning from our students than to hear directly from them about what is working, what they need, and what they suggest educators do to help foster learning and relationships. For this book, I queried former students and requested feedback on their experiences in my classroom (from 2008 to 2020). Hearing their perspective now, asking them to look back and reflect, and continuing to learn from their observations has allowed me to understand what practices and lessons resonated—to find out what worked and remained with them all these years later. I hope the questions I suggest here, and my former students' feedback, help guide your own effort to hear from and listen to your current students in your continuing endeavors to make them feel valued, affirmed, and heard.

BUILDING RELATIONSHIPS

I asked a selection of former students the following question: "What are some things that occurred in our classroom to enhance the learning content and/or build relationships that other teachers and classrooms could benefit from?" In the next sections, I share common themes that emerged from their feedback that align with the un/HUSH framework, and I highlight excerpts from their replies that may impact your own instructional decision-making. You will see that the stories they mentioned led to connection, the histories they discussed led to deeper realizations, and the healing they cited occurred through journaling. The chapter closes as I discuss my own unlearning that I experienced as I navigated the various needs and challenges each student faced.

Let Students Guide Discussions (Histories)

One way to truly center student voice is to do just that—to not only allow students to share their observations and experiences through discussion, but also allow them to *lead* discussions. Doing so builds their interpersonal skills and leadership skills, and offers them space to put inquiry-based learning into practice. Normalizing making time for discussion and reflection in the classroom has the potential to impact students' learning in profound ways.

> As a Muslim and a student, I learned early on to appreciate words. "If you have nothing good to say, it is better not to say anything." This is an essential concept in Islam, as there is great emphasis on the importance of speech and its impact on others. From a young age, I was encouraged to choose my words carefully, as every time a person opens their mouth to speak, they share what is in their heart. Thus, I became hyperaware of my chosen words, their power, and who was listening.
>
> Words are powerful. They can uplift or harm a person's spirit. They can inspire, motivate, and encourage individuals to strive to achieve their goals. Conversely, they can also discourage and often make someone feel insignificant. See, the potency of words lies in their capacity to shape our perception—either of ourselves or of others. They can sway our emotions and ultimately influence our actions and those around us.
>
> As a Black Muslim student, many people only considered one aspect of my identity for most of my formal education. My teachers and peers often assigned which aspect or form of my identity precludes the others. I remember trying to justify the dismissal of the intricacies of my identity by telling myself it was too complicated, too insignificant. However, in Mrs. Bunch's classroom, her focus was never just on what we could see but also on what we could share. She often would tell us to pay attention to the vocabulary of a given text and prompt us about the intentionality of word choice. Her teaching style was centered mainly around creative writing, storytelling, introspection, and fostering our understanding of intersectional identities. She understood that who we were and what we looked like were not the same, and she gave us every opportunity to express ourselves. This made her classroom such a positive and engaging learning environment.
>
> —Munira, Former Student

> I think one of the key parts [of Mrs. Bunch's class] was discussion. Having a daily writing/discussion prompt was impactful. It created moments of vulnerability, which became a snowball effect and broke down walls. Students felt comfortable sharing relevant experiences and stories. Stories were validated and students were acknowledged and thanked when they would share their stories. Mrs. Bunch was not afraid to spend a lot of time with journals and discussion when people had

> meaningful things to share. One thing that enhanced learning content with engagement is she would preview things or let us know about the fun we would have. Showing examples of final projects from former students before we started, giving us little pieces of "we will get to do *x*" always made me very excited to learn—I understood that there would be engaging activities attached to my learning from the start.
>
> —Gage, Former Student and Current Teacher

Socratic Seminar Reflection Activity

Like Gage, many educators will be familiar with the Socratic seminar activity, where students help one another understand the ideas, issues, and values reflected in a text through a group discussion format where *students* are responsible for facilitating the conversation. Several of my former students mentioned the importance of dialogue, guided conversations, and Socratic seminars as ways they felt listened to in my classroom. Figure 5.1 walks you through how to engage in Socratic seminars that connect with the un/HUSH framework.

Take a moment to brainstorm a list of what other information you want or need to consider before implementing a Socratic seminar. Question stems to help guide your first Socratic seminar activity are listed below.

Socratic Seminar Questions Using the un/HUSH Framework

- **(H) Histories:** What histories exist in this discussion? What histories might be overlooked? Whose histories are celebrated? Where can you find examples of the above within the text?
- **(U) Unlearning:** What unlearning needs to occur related to this topic? How do we best approach that unlearning process?
- **(S) Stories:** What role do stories play in the text? Why are they important? What can you infer from them?
- **(H) Healing:** How can this topic and discussion lead us toward a deeper understanding of one another? Tell me more about how the text approaches concepts related to healing. What text/self or text/world connections can you make?

Figure 5.1. Socratic Seminar Implementation Guide

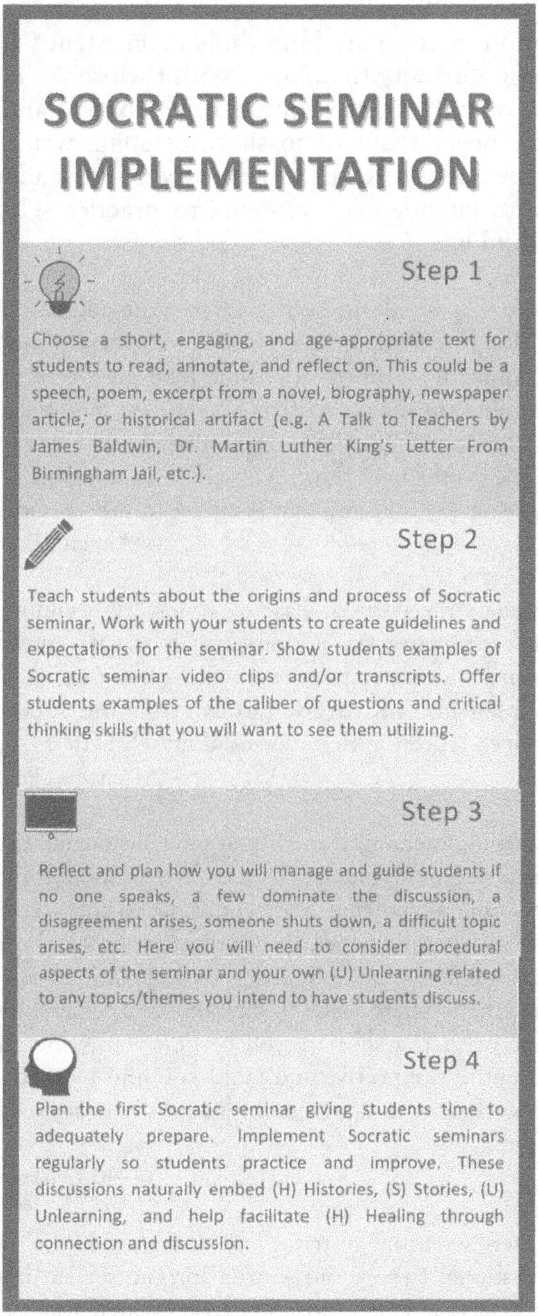

Encourage Journaling as a Personal Space (Stories)

Journaling and reflection are both tools I consistently use to allow students the opportunity to connect with themselves and to begin forming their own thoughts about learning content and the world. Students were never required to share personal writing, as these moments of personal safe space were free from grading or judgment and were intended for students to practice self-assessment and critical thinking.

> I appreciate that we all took the time to write and had the option to share out loud. It made me think, and still does to this day. It also made me think about other people and their perspective or what they might be going through, and that maybe you might share the same struggles. It helped me realize how similar we all are, and that sometimes people go through things you couldn't imagine. It showed me that you are never alone and that someone out there understands you.
>
> —Angelo, Former Student

> One of my favorite parts of class was the very beginning where you had a timer for us to write in our journals about a question you had on the board or connected to something were going to do during class. It felt like my only part of the day I truly was at peace and made space for deep reflection to understand myself better.
>
> —Michaela, Former Student

> Nightly writing, it changed my life. It gave me a true love of writing, which has lasted in my life to this day. The random topics you chose always gave me a challenge and taught me to think critically. More than putting a pen to paper, but really putting my heart and mind into what I was writing. I still have the composition book I used back then. Also, the letter to self.[1] It was amazing to see how much you can change in such a short period of time. How life and its events shift your entire perspective and mold you into who you've become. If only it worked in reverse, the things I'd say to myself back then if only I could.
>
> —Katie, Former Student

> You definitely set a tone of trust, and students felt like they were safe to ask questions. I think our journal prompts were important and great for students. The atmosphere you created was safe and comforting; I don't know how you teach that. You made a clear effort to

> value each student as an individual. Your classroom was a safe place to share experiences, learn, and gain exposures to other experiences.
>
> —Cassidy, Former Student

Letter to Self Activity

At the start of each school year, I would ask students to write a letter to themselves. The letter could say anything they wanted, and the only request was that they draft their initial thoughts before writing the final version of their letter. I would then collect the letters and return them to the students at the end of the school year. This activity allowed them to not only reflect on but also witness their growth both personally and academically. Try this activity in your own classroom to have students reflect on their lives and experiences.

Another version of this activity is to share the poem "Theme for English B" by Langston Hughes with the class and then ask students to write a letter to you, modeling the format of Hughes's poem. Doing an activity such as this, especially at the start of the school year, is a good way to gain an understanding of the students' writing, begin learning about them, and build connections.

Writing Reflection Activity

Writing activities can be incorporated into any subject or grade level. Consider how you can offer low-stakes writing opportunities, such as bell work (brief activities at the start of the class for 5–10 minutes) or journaling, with your students to help encourage their storytelling and their investment in writing. Think about ways you can allow students to consider counterarguments, other perspectives, and stories in the content area you teach through writing. How can you use journaling prompts to make writing accessible and offer students a chance to pause and reflect? A few writing strategies that work for most subjects include creative writing, journaling, poetry, and travel journals.

Now, take a moment to start a list of some writing prompts that align with your grade level, subject, and the principles of the un/HUSH framework. Below, you'll find a list of some examples I have used with my students. They wrote every night, and I called it "nightly writing." These prompts are not intended to be used for assessment purposes or to be shared out loud with the class. They are for the student only and are meant to allow students the space to think through topics without judgment and to help instill a joy of writing and reflection. Encourage your students to write every day, to keep a journal, and to look back at previous entries from time to time.

Student Journal Prompts

(UN) Uniting for Collective Effort and Naming Your Positionality

- If you could collaborate with anyone, who would it be and what would you hope to accomplish by working with them?
- Discuss an aspect of your positionality that greatly informs your view of the world.

(H) Histories

- If you could have dinner with anyone alive or deceased, who would it be, where would you go, what would you say?
- Discuss a choice you have made and its impact.
- What are you most proud of?
- Discuss one thing you would like to achieve or accomplish.
- Discuss one topic that you believe teachers should be more informed about.
- When/where do you feel most like yourself?
- What are our social and global responsibilities?
- What history or time period do you wish you knew more about?

(U) Unlearning

- Name and explain one thing you would change about school or learning.
- Self-evaluation: What is good? What needs improvement?
- Discuss one preconceived idea you have and examine it.
- Free write about anything you want to resolve or clear your mind about.

(S) Stories

- What part of the world would you most like to see and why?
- Discuss a person or event that has impacted you.
- What if . . . ?
- What is a song that best represents you and why?
- What is the biggest issue facing young people/teens today?

- Think through your story. Write about it.

(H) Healing

- If you could relive one day or moment, what would it be and why?
- Write a letter to anyone.
- I've always wanted to say . . .
- Discuss one thing you would like to overcome.
- How can you work with another person or group to improve a societal concern that matters to you?
- What inspires you? What brings you joy?
- Discuss the last time you did something nice for someone and expected nothing in return.

Connect and Empathize With Students (Healing)

Vulnerability and empathy are both key aspects to building and sustaining culturally responsive classrooms. Empathy is a word we hear often, and it truly is a fundamental aspect of facilitating healing and connection. Empathy is a key component to building a classroom that has respect, trust, and effective communication—all of which allow students to feel comfortable expressing their ideas, exploring unknown topics, and asking for guidance when needed.

> You connected with students and listened. You helped me feel heard when my home life was in shambles. I feel that is a big part of what a lot of teachers miss the mark on. You gave us the room to make mistakes and to make our own choices but reminded us that there are consequences and outcomes to what we choose.
>
> —Terriah, Former Student

> Overall, the one-on-one time and connections you made with each student mattered so much—getting to know students beyond what you saw or heard in just the hour you had them. Your teaching helped us identify our weaknesses and make them our strengths. You pushed us to do better and provided a safe haven for students to be themselves. This helped us go into a classroom and connect with others who may not look like us but allowed us to come together as one. You made us want to learn.
>
> —Miyah, Former Student

> Something you did in the classroom to enhance the learning and/or build relationships was having us write in journals every day when class started. I still have a regular habit of journaling today solely because of that class. It's been amazing for my mental health, even before I knew what mental health was.
>
> —Marcus, Former Student

> Typically, art classes consist of mirroring techniques with brushes and clay to express elements of creativity. For me, my art class was Mrs. Bunch's classroom, where I flourished in my personal expression of writing. I never uncovered the power of words until I experienced the power of Mrs. Bunch's. Her perspective transformed how I viewed the world and finally saw my own reflection in it. I was awakened to my own autonomy and how I was a small piece that fit into the merging mosaics of every current event happening around me. Being understood by someone with so much wisdom inspired me to respond to questions I never knew existed yet were staring me in my face all along. For the first time, I encountered a deep level of vulnerability that led to calls of responsibility.
>
> —Michaela, Former Student

Thinking Beyond the Lesson (Unlearning)

Every educator has the journey of unlearning. My own unlearning has been sparked by the experiences I have had with students. I have had to unlearn the idea of what it means to have "control" in the classroom, and the notion that a "good" classroom is a quiet one. Most effective lessons and learning that I have witnessed were far from quiet and instead were filled with the noise of students talking, laughing, or reacting to content. Those moments often required me to abandon control and let go of a daily plan or timeline I intended. Doing so allowed me to take more time on a topic or unit, reteach a concept, and so forth.

Additionally, I have always had to remind myself of the messages from my own school experiences regarding what academic potential and readiness look like. I unlearned this notion through experiences and while working on my degree in gifted education. Students' grades are not always indicative of their commitment, interest, potential, or existing knowledge. Learning is more than what we have reduced it to and should involve knowledge that relates to real-world learning. I have worked to unlearn that only the students in the schools I typically taught in (the Title I, more diverse schools) need culturally responsive teachers. I learned that students in *all schools* need invested teachers and the representation of Black and Brown educators.

Finally, I had to unlearn what I had thought being a teacher meant and relearn what being a *lighthouse* teacher means and looks like (teaching as a guide, not as the primary voice in the classroom). I had to be willing to give up control and trust my students if I wanted to have a classroom built on the notion that effective teaching and learning are done in community alongside others. These are just a few of the many lessons I have learned throughout my own unlearning and relearning.

Take a moment to recall some of your own transformative moments in the classroom. What were they? What helped cultivate those positive results?

Throughout my teaching, I witnessed students grow. Witnessing their lives has been an incredible honor. They taught me that education is about guiding and listening, and because of them I became a lighthouse teacher. They inspired me to want to learn more and become a better educator. They made me want to create lessons that worked to enrich their lives in the same way that they enriched mine. Their memories of our classroom may be glorified in some ways, as I certainly made mistakes as an educator, but what remained constant was the goal of creating a classroom that opened some small space for each student, and making sure it was filled with a blend of learning and love.

SOLICITING STUDENT FEEDBACK

Listening to your students' feedback, and teaching them how to offer worthwhile feedback, can be valuable to your growth as an educator. Throughout my teaching I have sought out my students' feedback regarding lessons, activities, and teaching approaches. Use the prompts below to create your own end-of-semester or end-of-year assessment form:

1. Please share what occurred this year that positively impacted your learning and growth.
2. Share with me some of the ways I was able to meet your learning needs this year. Offer specific examples.
3. Share with me aspects that I can improve upon. Be specific, be tactful.

4. Do you believe I demonstrated an investment in you and your learning? Explain.
5. Describe our classroom environment from your lens. What worked, what didn't?
6. Did our classroom incorporate histories, unlearning, stories? Did it foster healing? Did these aspects enhance your learning? If so, how? If not, explain why.
7. Did this class allow you to explore yourself, others, the community, and a wide range of diverse perspectives?
8. List two of your favorite lessons or activities, and tell why you felt they were important. What lesson or activity was missing that you would have added?

Listening to students and leveraging them as a resource for your own development can be instrumental in creating a classroom that has lasting impact for students.

My students' recollections and advice affirm the power of writing, discussion, and a classroom that prioritizes building relationships and a sense of community. These are the practices and aspects of curriculum that stayed with them after all these years and were a catalyst for future endeavors. While seemingly simple practices, they can help create lifelong skills: social skills, literacy skills, and most importantly a sense of self that will stay with them throughout their lives and make evident the many gifts they possessed all along.

Preservice Teacher Guidance

Some of the best guidance I can offer to preservice and new teachers is to build relationships with students and families. This likely sounds overly optimistic and trite, but it is the single most effective and meaningful aspect I have seen in teaching. It sounds easy, but building authentic relationships with hundreds of students each year is not an easy task. So how do you do it? Ask your students questions, listen, create assignments that naturally allow you insights into who they are and into their lives, reach out to parents, and treat your students with equal respect and care. Find one thing you admire about each of your students. At the beginning of each year, I would write postive traits and words in the margins of my attendance list that I printed off for each student. On difficult days, this was also helpful in reminding me of the initial beauty I saw in each student. Avoid asking for or listening to other teachers' assessments or judgments about students, because each student deserves a clean slate each year. What one teacher experiences with a student may not be same as what you experience. Use proximity to foster relationships, manage classroom behaviors, and prevent discipline issues. This might look like how you arrange your classroom desks. I always preferred a circle or pods (a few desks grouped togther)—this helped establish the norm that we are equally engaged and present in this classroom space. Take the time to meet with students one-to-one. Attend your students' games, plays, dances, and so on. Being present at some of your school's events shows students your investment in their lives and interests beyond academics. Write your students a quick note of encouragement, organize or lead a club related to your students' interests, and most importantly be willing to share aspects of yourself in return. Keep in mind that building relationships should not be equated to whether or not a student likes you. Not all students will like you, some connections will not be long lasting, and there might be some students who are not interested in building relationships in the classroom, and that is OK—just be another adult who will show them respect and care. Positive relationships in the classroom have the potential to change their lives—and also yours. Be a mentor and a role model, and the relationships will come in time. Students have a keen sense of knowing who is in their corner.

PAUSE AND REFLECT

- How will you center and listen to students' voices? How can the physical space of your classroom support this? How can the relationships in your classroom support this? How can the curriculum and lessons support amplifying student voice?
- Name two pieces of advice offered in Chapter 5 that resonated with you and explain why.
- What would you add or contribute to any of the lists offered in Chapter 5?
- What concerns or hesitations exist when we center students' voices and/or stories? How can you alleviate

those concerns? How can you effectively listen to and validate students' voices?

- How do you handle the hardest parts of teaching? What are some of your go-to strategies to get through the hard parts?
- What are your teaching superpowers? How do these strengths most benefit your classroom and students?
- What superpowers do you still hope to develop or obtain, and how could they enhance your classroom?

Epilogue

> I leave you love. I leave you hope. I leave you the challenge of developing confidence in one another.
>
> —Mary McLeod Bethune

We can sometimes lose sight of the importance of the histories and efforts that came before us. Currently, we are challenged with issues that are cyclical. This alone is enough to prompt a reminder regarding the importance of history and of holding the ground that was fought for by earlier generations. As we navigate voting rights, racism, women's rights, book bans, inequitable policies, and other societal struggles, it is imperative that we study the lessons of the past and document the efforts from years ago.

The classroom is a powerful place to connect our past to our present—offering lessons for tomorrow. These legacies and lessons are important and relevant, and they are timely, considering all we face today. The word *sankofa* aptly describes this sentiment and translates to "it is not taboo to fetch what is at risk of being left behind." This word from the Akan tribe in Ghana reminds us that if we are going to imagine a better future, we must consider the lessons of our past and seek the guidance of lessons learned yesterday. Tomorrow can be better if we look back and fetch what happened yesterday.

Figure E.1. Sankofa Bird

The appendices at the end of this book will help you utilize the un/HUSH framework and create culturally responsive lessons and activities for your students.

Afterword

Toward Action

The first time I taught in a classroom, I was eighteen and nervous. I had just completed my first year as an English and education double major at Smith College in Northampton, Massachusetts, and I had agreed to spend a portion of my summer living on campus as a residential teaching assistant in a precollege summer writing program for female-identifying high school students. I was besotted by my vision of one day becoming an English teacher, poring over the power of poetry and prose with my students—so much so that I often annotated the pages of my pleasure reading with ideas for lessons or classroom activities. The opportunity to support a classroom experience, hold office hours, and help students study during dorm duty seemed like the perfect start.

There were many things I did not know that summer. I did not know that I would walk into that brick building and meet Dr. Marlee Bunch, who would not only affirm and extend my visions for education but also become a lifelong collaborator and friend. I did not know that we would create a community of writers dedicated to advocating for social change through the written word, sharing pieces of their identity at local poetry slams and through our culminating class publication. And I didn't know that I was about to experience a powerful pedagogy that would change the lives of teen writers.

Witnessing Marlee in the classroom is like watching a painter perfect their brushstrokes, so intentional is she in her approaches to engagement, empowerment, and equitable instruction. She is the first to wave her arms in celebration of a student's narrated poetry, to validate and center a student's challenging lived experience shared in the safe space of her classroom, to share with students the names of historical activists as if passing out song recommendations. Pivotal yet minoritized changemakers come to life in her classroom, as if sitting in desks alongside her, as she simultaneously believes into being her own students' abilities to become advocates and activists through learning. In Marlee's teaching, I hear the echoes of ancestors and mentors whose alchemy paved the way.

Unhushed means moving—through pedagogy and instructional planning—toward the deepest elements of education: compassion, self-reflection, perspective-taking, critical analysis. It means challenging assumptions and positionalities. And it means believing in the power of story to make a difference, to sew the first patch in a quilt of awakened understanding.

Teaching with Marlee in the first days of my career, I watched as a student who was reluctant to contribute to class discussions became enraptured with writing, typing stanzas on their iPhone to perform aloud at a public reading, giving voice to their testimony—their identity and vision for the future. In this one young person was a microcosm of impact representative of the change that Marlee's pedagogy and framework make manifest. I invite you to join me in embracing the un/HUSH framework—in becoming unhushed—to embrace coalition, to stand up and speak out for equity and justice and school as a space for change, and to spread this approach far and wide so that young writers, scholars, and changemakers might see the first spark of their future selves ignited in the classroom.

In solidarity,
Brittany R. Collins
Educator and Author

Endnotes

Chapter 2

1. Eliot Eisner's explicit curricula, implicit curricula, and null curricula apply. The framework encourages us to consider the null curricula and challenge those silences, while also taking into account the explicit curricula.

Chapter 4

1. Evie Shockley, "good night women (or, defying the carcinogenic pen)" from *The New Black*, 2012. Published by Wesleyan University Press. Used with permission.
2. Ashley M. Jones, poet laureate of Alabama.
3. Cole Swensen, poet. This poem first appeared in *Gravesend* and has been printed here with the author's and publisher's permission.

Chapter 5

1. The letter to self was an assignment that I had students complete at the start of the year. I kept their letters and then gave them back to the students at the end of the school year so they could see their growth and change.

References

Abd-El-Khalick, F., Boujaoude, S., Duschl, R., Lederman, N. G., Mamlok-Naaman, R., Hofstein, A., Niaz, M., Treagust, D., & Tuan, H. (2004). Inquiry in science education: International perspectives. *Science Education, 88*(3), 397–419.

Abdi, A. (2014). The effect of inquiry-based learning method on students' academic achievement in science course. *Universal Journal of Educational Research, 2*(1), 37–41.

Ahmad, F., & Boser, U. (2014). *America's leaky pipeline for teachers of color: Getting more teachers of color into the classroom.* Center for American Progress.

Akinbode, A. (2013). Teaching as lived experience: The value of exploring the hidden and emotional side of teaching through reflective narratives. *Studying Teacher Education, 9*(1), 62–73. https://doi.org/10.1080/17425964.2013.771574

Albert Shanker Institute. (2015). *The state of teacher diversity in American education.* https://www.shankerinstitute.org/resource/state-teacher-diversity-american-education

Alridge, D. P., Bynum, C. L., Stewart, J. B., Blain, K. N., Coleman, J. L., Dagbovie, P. G., Evans, S. Y., Gresson, A. D., Harold, C. N., & Harris, L. (2021). *The Black intellectual tradition: African American thought in the twentieth century.* University of Illinois Press.

Anderson, D. S. (2017). *Emmett Till: The murder that shocked the world and propelled the civil rights movement.* University Press of Mississippi.

Aspelin, J. (2021). Teaching as a way of bonding: A contribution to the relational theory of teaching. *Educational Philosophy and Theory, 53*(6), 588–596.

Ball, A. F., & Tyson, C. A. (Eds.). (2011). *Studying diversity in teacher education.* Rowman & Littlefield.

Ball, E. L., & Lai, A. (2006, April). Place-based pedagogy for the arts and humanities. *Pedagogy,* 6(2), 261–287.

Bonilla, S., Dee, T. S., & Penner, E. K. (2021). Ethnic studies increases longer-run academic engagement and attainment. *PNAS: Proceedings of the National Academy of Sciences of the United States of America, 118*(37), e2026386118. https://www.pnas.org/content/118/37/e2026386118

Borden, J. D. (2021, August 4). *The neuroscience of unlearning*. Cengage. https://todayslearner.cengage.com/the-neuroscience-of-unlearning/

Boutte, G. S., Johnson, G. L., Wynter-Hoyt, K., & Uyoata, U. E. (2017). Using African diaspora literacy to heal and restore the souls of Black folks. *International Critical Childhood Policy Studies Journal*, 6(1), 66–79.

Breslin, A. K., Dahlen, S. P., Kwisnek, K., & Leathersich, B. (2021). *APALA rubric to evaluate Asian American and Pacific Islander youth literature*. APALA: Asian/Pacific American Librarians Association. https://www.apalaweb.org/talkstorytogether/resources/apala-youth-literature-evaluation-rubric/

Brooks, G. (2005). *The essential Gwendolyn Brooks*. Library of America.

Bunch, M. (2023, September 29). Lessons for today from the overlooked stories of Black teachers during the segregated civil rights era. *The Conversation*. https://theconversation.com/lessons-for-today-from-the-overlooked-stories-of-black-teachers-during-the-segregated-civil-rights-era-213811

CBS News. (2016, September 12). *Ava DuVernay on significance of August 28 in black history* [Video]. YouTube https://www.youtube.com/watch?v=fTvialHngrcfTvialHngrc

Chang, V. (2021). *Dear memory: Letters on writing, silence, and grief*. Milkweed Editions.

Cohen, D., & Crabtree, B. (2006). *Qualitative research guidlines*. Project Robert Wood Johnson Foundation. http://www.qualres.org/HomeRefl-3703.html

Collins, B. (2021). *Learning from loss: A trauma-informed approach to supporting grieving students*. Heinemann.

Cron, L. (2012). *Wired for story: The writer's guide to using brain science to hook readers from the very first sentence*. Ten Speed.

Dantas, M. L. (2007). Building teacher competency to work with diverse learners in the context of international education. *Teacher Education Quarterly*, *34*(1), 79–94.

Davenport, M. (2000). Culture and education: Polishing the lenses. *Studies in Art Education*, *41*(4), 361–375.

Delacruz, E. M., Arnold, A., Kuo, A., & Parsons, M. (Eds.). (2009). *Globalization, art, and education*. National Art Education Association.

DeNicolo, C. P., & Gonzalez, M. (2015). *Testimoniando* en Nepantla: Using *testimonio* as a pedagogical tool for exploring embodied literacies and bilingualism. *Journal of Language and Literacy Education*, *11*(1), 109–126.

Dutro, E. (2019). *The vulnerable heart of literacy*. Teachers College Press.

Dutt-Doner, K. M., Allen, S., & Campanaro, K. (2016). Understanding the impact of using oral histories in the classroom. *The Social Studies*, *107*(6), 257–265. https://doi.org/10.1080/00377996.2016.1221792

Ehret, C., & Leander, K. (2019). Introduction. In K. Leander & C. Ehret (Eds.), *Affect in literacy learning and teaching: Pedagogies, politics and coming to know* (pp. 1–19). Routledge. https://doi.org/10.4324/9781351256766-1

Eisner, E. (2002). *The arts and the creation of mind*. Yale University Press.

Fairclough, A. (2007). *A class of their own: Black teachers in the segregated South*. Belknap Press.

Forché, C. (Ed.). (1993). *Against forgetting: Twentieth-century poetry of witness*. W. W. Norton.

Fox, D., & Short, K. (2003). *Stories matter: The complexity of cultural authenticity in children's literature*. National Council of Teachers of English.

Frost, E. (2019). A perspective on positionality. In A. Blakeslee & C. Fleisher (Eds.), *Becoming a writing researcher* (pp. 44–46). Routledge.

Gay, G. (2000). *Culturally responsive teaching: Theory, research, and practice*. Teachers College Press.

Gay, G., & Kirkland, K. (2003). Developing cultural critical consciousness and self-reflection in preservice teacher education. *Theory Into Practice*, *42*(3), 181–187. http://www.jstor.org/stable/1477418

Gere, A. R., Buehler, J., Dallavis, C., & Haviland, V. S. (2009). A visibility project: Learning to see how preservice teachers take up culturally responsive pedagogy. *American Educational Research Journal*, *46*(3), 816–852. http://www.jstor.org/stable/40284863

Ghiso, M. P., & Low, D. E. (2013). Students using multimodal literacies to surface micro narratives of United States immigration. *Literacy*, *47*, 26–34.

Goldin, S., & Khasnabis, D. (2021). In the pursuit of justice: Moving past color-evasive efforts. *The Educational Forum*, *86*(1), 1–4. https://doi.org/10.1080/00131725.2022.1997307

Griffin, A. R., Dixon, R. D., & Tackie, H. N. (2022). Perspectives of Black teachers' experiences in the field and the connection to retention. In C. D. Gist & T. J. Bristol (Eds.), *Handbook of research on teachers of color and Indigenous teachers* (pp. 909–922). American Educational Research Association. https://doi.org/10.2307/j.ctv2xqngb9.69

Hammond, Z. (2015). *Culturally responsive teaching and the brain: Promoting authentic engagement and rigor among culturally and linguistically diverse students*. Corwin.

Hammond, Z. (2020). The power of protocols for equity. *Educational Leadership*, *77*(7), 45–50.

Handsfield, L. J., & Valente, P. (2016) Momentos de cambio: Cultivating bilingual students' epistemic privilege through memoir and testimonio. *International Journal of Multicultural Education*, *18*, 138–158.

Hawkins, D. (2007). *The informed vision: Essays on learning and human nature*. Algora Publishing. (Original work published 1974)

Hines, E., & Hines, M. (2020, August 11). Want to support Black students? Invest in Black teachers. *Time*. https://time.com/5876164/black-teachers/

hooks, b. (2003). *Teaching community*. Psychology Press.

Hudson, M. J., & Holmes, B. J. (1994). Missing teachers, impaired communities: The unanticipated consequences of *Brown v. Board of Education* on the African American teaching force at the pre-collegiate level. *The Journal of Negro Education*, *63*, 388–393. https://doi.org/10.2307/2967189

Hyland, N. E. (2005). Being a good teacher of Black students? White teachers and unintentional racism. *Curriculum Inquiry*, *35*(4), 429–459.

Ingersoll, R., & May, H. (2016). *Minority teacher recruitment, employment, and retention: 1987 to 2013* [Research brief]. Learning Policy Institute.

Irvine, J. J. (2003). *Educating teachers for diversity: Seeing with a cultural eye*. Teachers College Press.

Ketelle, D. (2017). Introduction to the special issue: What is storytelling in the higher education classroom? *Storytelling, Self, Society*, *13*(2), 143–150. https://doi.org/10.13110/storselfsoci.13.2.0143

Koch, K. (1990). *Rose, where did you get that red? Teaching great poetry to children*. Vintage. (Original work published 1973)

Koch, K. (1999). *Making your own days: The pleasures of reading and writing poetry*. Touchstone.

Kohli, R. (2018). Behind school doors: The impact of hostile racial climates on urban teachers of color. *Urban Education*, *53*(3), 307–333.

Kohli, R. (2019). Lessons for teacher education: The role of critical professional development in teacher of Color retention. *Journal of Teacher Education, 70*(1), 39–50. https://doi.org/10.1177/0022487118767645

Kohli, R., & Pizarro, M. (2016). Fighting to educate our own: Teachers of color, relational accountability, and the struggle for racial justice. *Equity & Excellence in Education*, *49*(1), 72–84.

Krug, D., & Parker, A. (2009). A journal of critical inquiry and professional learning: Telling tales of community art, aesthetics, and cultures. *Art Education*, *62*(4), 33–40.

Ladner, J. A. (1995). *Tomorrow's tomorrow: The Black woman*. University of Nebraska Press.

Ladner, J. A. (2000). A new civil rights agenda. *The Brookings Review*, *18*(2), 26–28. https://doi.org/10.2307/20080906

Ladner, J. (2012). Standing up for our beliefs. In F. S. Holsaert, M. P. N. Noonan, J. Richardson, B. G. Robinson, J. S. Young, & D. M. Zellner (Eds.), *Hands on the freedom plow: Personal accounts by women in SNCC* (pp. 217–223). University of Illinois Press.

Ladson-Billings, G. (1994). *The dreamkeepers: Successful teachers of African American children*. Jossey-Bass.

Ladson-Billings, G. (2014). Culturally relevant pedagogy 2.0: a.k.a. The remix. *Harvard Educational Review*, *84*(1), 74–84. https://doi.org/10.17763/haer.84.1.p2rj131485484751

Ladson-Billings, G. (2022). *The dreamkeepers: Successful teachers of African American children*. John Wiley & Sons, Inc.

Lasky, D., Luxford, D., & Nathan, J. (2013). *Open the door: How to excite young people about poetry*. McSweeney's Books.

Lewis, A. E. (2001). There is no "race" in the schoolyard: Color-blind ideology in an (almost) all-white school. *American Educational Research Journal, 38*(4), 781–811.

Love, B. (2020). *We want to do more than survive: Abolitionist teaching and the pursuit of educational freedom*. Beacon Press.

Ludwig, M., Kirshstein, R., Sidana, A., Ardila-Rey, A., & Bae, Y. (2010). *An emerging picture of the teacher preparation pipeline: A report by the American Association of Colleges for Teacher Education and the American Institutes for Research for release at the briefing: Teacher preparation: Who needs it? What the numbers say*. American Association of Colleges for Teacher Education and American Institutes for Research.

Lyman, H. (2006). I-Search in the age of information. *English Journal, 95*(4), 62–67.

Mace, D. (2014). Galvanizing the Emmett Till generation. In *In remembrance of Emmett Till: Regional stories and media responses to the Black freedom struggle* (pp. 95–132). University Press of Kentucky. http://www.jstor.org/stable/j.ctt6wrs7n.10

Macrorie, K. (1998). *The I-Search paper: Revised edition of* Searching writing. Heinemann-Boynton/Cook.

McAllister, G., & Irvine, J. J. (2000). Cross cultural competency and multicultural teacher education. *Review of Educational Research, 70*(1), 3–24. https://www.jstor.org/stable/1170592

Milner, H. R. (2007). Race, culture, and researcher positionality: Working through dangers seen, unseen, and unforeseen. *Educational Researcher, 36*(7), 388–400. http://www.jstor.org/stable/30136070

Muhammad, G. (2023). *Unearthing joy*. Scholastic.

Nadworny, E. (2015, April 24). *Uncomfortable conversations: Talking about race in the classroom*. National Public Radio. https://www.npr.org/sections/ed/2015/04/24/401214280/uncomfortable-conversations-talking-about-race-in-the-classroom

National Center for Education Statistics. (2010). *Digest of education statistics: 2009*. NCES 2010-013. Department of Education, Institute of Education Sciences. https://nces.ed.gov/programs/digest/d09/

National Center for Education Statistics. (2023). *Public high school graduation rates*. U.S. Department of Education, Institute of Education Sciences. https://nces.ed.gov/programs/coe/indicator/coi

Navarro, S. B., Zervas, P., Gesa, R. F., & Sampson, D. G. (2016). Developing teachers' competences for designing inclusive learning experiences. *Journal of Educational Technology & Society, 19*(1), 17–27. http://www.jstor.org/stable/jeductechsoci.19.1.17

Pacheco, M. (2009). Expansive learning and Chicana/o and Latina/o students' political-historical knowledge. *Language Arts*, *87*(1), 18–29.

Padgett, R. (Ed.). (2007). *The teachers & writers handbook of poetic forms* (2nd ed.). Teachers & Writers Collaborative.

Paris, D., Alim, H. S., Kinloch, V., Bucholtz, M., Casillas, D. I., Lee, J.-S., Lee, T. S., McCarty, T. L., Irizarry, J. G., Pedro, S. T., Wong, C., Peña, C., Ladson-Billings, G., Haupt, A., Rosa, J., Flores, N., Lee, S. J., González, N., Gutiérrez, K. D., . . . Lee, C. D. (2017). *Culturally sustaining pedagogies: Teaching and learning for justice in a changing world.* Teachers College Press.

Perry, A. (2020, May 26). The educational value of a Black teacher. *The Hechinger Report.* https://hechingerreport.org/the-educational-value-of-a-black-teacher/

Richmond, E. (2012, June 11). Schools are more segregated today than during the late 1960s. *The Atlantic.* https://www.theatlantic.com/national/archive/2012/06/schools-are-more-segregated-today-than-during-the-late-1960s/258348/

Sellers, C. (2013, March 21). *Cleveland Sellers oral history interview conducted by John Dittmer in Denmark, South Carolina, 2013 March 21* [Video]. Civil Rights History Project (U.S.). https://www.loc.gov/item/2015669180/

Short, K. G. (2012). Story as world making. *Language Arts*, *90*(1), 9–17. http://www.jstor.org/stable/41804370

Siddle Walker, V. (2000). Valued segregated schools for African American children in the South, 1935–1969: A review of common themes and characteristics. *Review of Educational Research*, *70*(3), 253–285. https://doi.org/10.3102/00346543070003253

Sims Bishop, R. (1990). Mirrors, windows, and sliding glass doors. *Perspectives: Choosing and Using Books From the Classroom*, *6*(3), ix–xi. https://scenicregional.org/wp-content/uploads/2017/08/Mirrors-Windows-and-Sliding-Glass-Doors.pdf

Sleeter, C., & Zavala, M. (2020). *Transformative ethnic studies in schools: Curriculum, pedagogy, and research.* Teachers College Press.

Tamari, F., & Ho, I. S. (2019). Guided inquiry-based activities positively impact learning in community college courses. *Journal of College Science Teaching*, *48*(4), 12–21. https://www.jstor.org/stable/26901293

Venet, A. S. (2021). *Equity-centered trauma-informed education.* W. W. Norton.

Villegas, A. M., & Irvine, J. J. (2010). Diversifying the teaching force: An examination of major arguments. *The Urban Review*, *42*(3), 175–192. https://doi.org/10.1007/s11256-010-0150-1

Whitman, G. (2000). Teaching students how to be historians: An oral history project for the secondary school classroom. *The History Teacher*, *33*(4), 469–481. https://doi.org/10.2307/494943

Wineburg, S., Mosborg, S., Porat, D., & Duncan, A. (2007). Common belief and the cultural curriculum: An intergenerational study of historical consciousness. *American Educational Research Journal*, *44*(1), 40–76. https://doi.org/10.3102/0002831206298677

Zirkel, S. (2005). Ongoing issues of racial and ethnic stigma in education 50 years after *Brown v. Board*. *The Urban Review*, *37*(2), 107–126. https://doi.org/10.1007/s11256-005-0004-4

APPENDIX A

Guide to Using Oral Histories in the Classroom

Primary sources and oral histories are meaningful ways to introduce students to history, storytelling, and research. Inquiry-based learning can help guide students through archival material, primary source documents, and historical information to lead them to a more robust understanding of historical moments, figures, and occurrences not readily taught. Inquiry-based learning can be done through structured, controlled, guided or free inquiry, and all are intended to help students make meaningful connections in their learning (Abdi, 2014; Tamari & Ho, 2019; Whitman, 2000).

Teaching students how to use primary resources is an important precursor to helping them understand the power of oral histories and research. To begin introducing students to primary sources, first determine a guiding question that you would like students to consider (e.g., "what local efforts in the 1960s helped secure voting rights for Black communities?")

Next, compile a list of primary sources related to a historical topic/event/person that you wish to introduce your class to. You will want to offer students an overview and knowledge about what primary sources are, what they consist of, and how they can be used to excavate knowledge and information. You then show students various examples of primary sources. For example, Source A might be a historical photograph; Source B, the transcript from an interview; and Source C, a video clip. This activity can be set up in stations, as a jigsaw, in small groups, and so forth. The goal of all of this is to offer students the chance to identify and explore primary sources, collect information about the topic, and ask questions that unearth further discoveries.

Students will construct a visual and/or written response with the information they have discovered. This might be in the form of a mini-presentation, a short paper, a creative method of presenting

Figure A.1. The Benefits of Oral Histories

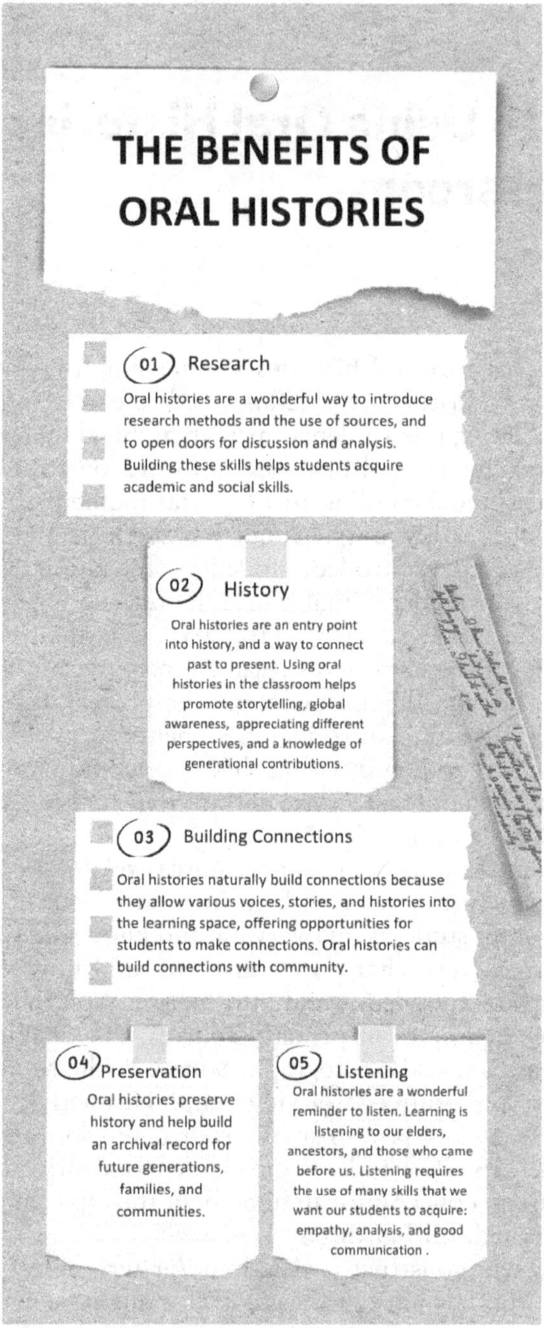

the information, or other means. This beginning project will lead students into the larger task of conducting an oral history interview to round out the information they have collected and to gain experience working with another example of a primary source (see Figure A.1). The guiding questions for the oral history interview may expand or shift.

What Skills Do Oral Histories Support?

- Listening
- Speaking
- Critical thinking and inquiry-based learning
- Synthesizing and compiling information
- Evaluating information and data
- Perspective taking
- Building intergenerational connections
- Building historical knowledge and context

STUDENT GUIDE TO ORAL HISTORIES

Students will have the option of listening to and/or conducting an oral history. Before listening to or conducting an oral history interview, you (the educator) will need to explain to students what oral history is and why it is important, offer examples of existing oral histories, help students craft meaningful interview questions, and give them guidelines for the process of evaluating the information they encounter and research. The list of questions that follows can be used to help students begin thinking about oral history interviews:

- What societal, social, and historical events shaped the narrator's perspective and life?
- How did the events they encountered or witnessed impact their life, career, identity, emotions, and so forth?
- What were some of the things the narrator described that stood out to you? Why?
- What did you learn from the oral history you encountered? What can we learn from this history?
- How can the narrator's story inform how we navigate challenges today?

- Reflect and discuss the differences between your life and the narrator's. What similarities exist? What differences exist? Do the similarities and/or differences tell us anything that we should consider?
- What benefits do oral histories allow us to experience?
- When we look back on the lives of others, what can we learn about intersectionality, identity, and duality?
- How might oral histories help us better understand communities and people that are not like us?

Lastly, allow students to share what they discovered and learned. Using oral histories in the classroom is a way to connect past to present, use stories to generate empathy, and create a broader picture of the histories and contributions that shape our world.

un/HUSH Framework Implementation Check-In Rubric

When implementing a new practice, we may wonder if we are doing it correctly. Are we consistently attempting to apply new practices and tools we have gained? Figure B.1 is a rubric to help you assess the level of implementation regarding the un/HUSH framework. Use it as a personal check-in or ask a co-teacher, paraprofessional, supervising teacher, or colleague you work with to help you assess the level of implementation of the framework.

Figure B.1. un/HUSH Self-Evaluation Tool

UN/HUSH SELF-EVALUATION

Use this form to self-evaluate implementation of the framework and culturally responsive and inclusive lessons.

HISTORIES

- ◯ Lessons illuminate histories not often told.
- ◯ Lessons demonstrate cultural and global awareness.
- ◯ Lessons ask and consider who is not included? Why?
- ◯ Students have opportunities to analyze history.
- ◯ We examine how current issues are rooted in the past.
- ◯ Histories are presented through a contemporary lens.
- ◯ Students have space to reflect & ask questions.
- ◯ We examine disparities/gaps in historical information.
- ◯ Lessons lean on lived experiences and oral histories to give voice to marginalized groups.

STORIES

- ◯ Lessons & activities include marginalized stories.
- ◯ I understand that stories build connection.
- ◯ I build stories into classroom lessons & activities.
- ◯ Our classroom works to acknowledge all stories.
- ◯ I use stories to make content & texts relevant.
- ◯ Lessons use stories to examine power dynamics.
- ◯ I elevate inclusive stories beyond calendar events.
- ◯ I use stories to reach instructional objectives.
- ◯ I use stories to forge connections and build relationships.

UNLEARNING

- ◯ Reflection & evaluation are part of my pre-planning.
- ◯ I seek out opportunities to learn and grow.
- ◯ Research is part of my curricular planning process.
- ◯ I regularly journal and consider difficult questions.
- ◯ I examine my own bias and gaps in knowledge.
- ◯ I consider how my positionality impacts my teaching.
- ◯ I seek to understand systemic barriers.
- ◯ I listen to others and seek to understand.
- ◯ I strive to be open-minded and accept feedback.

HEALING

- ◯ Lessons offer opportunities to build connections.
- ◯ Lessons foster empathy and perspective taking.
- ◯ Lessons encourage coalitions and civic engagement.
- ◯ Lessons offer choice and autonomy.
- ◯ Lessons explore action, agency & activism.
- ◯ Lessons offer varied perspectives.
- ◯ My classroom offers students choices in learning.

ADDITIONAL CONSIDERATIONS

- ◯ What do I want to learn more about?
- ◯ What new strategy am I willing to try?
- ◯ How does my positionality (lens) impact my classroom/lessons/students?
- ◯ What areas of growth should I consder?

https://www.marleebunch.com

Lesson Plan Examples

ELEMENTARY LESSON (GRADES 1–5)

Personal Power and Writing Structure

Special thanks to educator Amber Brutzkus for collaborating. Imagine that you want to create a lesson that can be used to teach the theme of personal power. You have an elementary classroom and are working on many reading and writing skills that need to be introduced and reinforced.

Lesson Title: Personal Power and Writing Structure

Lesson Description: This lesson is intended to teach character traits, use IRA (intentional read-alouds) to reinforce reading skills/ comprehension skills, expose students to various histories and perspectives, get students engaged with discourse opportunities, teach students about their personal power, and reinforce writing (structure: main idea and complete sentences).

Essential Question: How do the stories we tell ourselves shape our understanding of ourselves and others, and oftentimes create forms of bias and fallacies that prevent rational engagement with others and our thinking?

Learning Objectives: Analyze and evaluate reading and writing skills to build the foundation for lifelong readers, writers, and learners.

Aligned Illinois Common Core Standards: RL.1.3, RL.1.11, RI.1.7, RI.10, RF.1.1, W.1.2, W.1.7, W.1.8, SL.1.1, SL.1.5. Standards include speaking and listening, writing, and reading.

Materials/Instructional Resources:

- Poster(s) and instruction to teach and reinforce adjectives and writing structure
- Storybooks for three individuals. In this lesson we use Ruby Bridges, Jean-Michel Basquiat, and Naomi Osaka. Supplemental materials for the individuals used (e.g., short videos, additional books, etc.).
- Large paper (craft paper), markers, paint, crayons
- Historical materials and information for the teacher to offer an overview of the time period/persons

Instructional Strategies and Learning Tasks: This lesson would ideally occur over several days and could be built out into a larger unit.

Core Components of the un/HUSH Framework:

(H) Histories/History:

- Begin lesson by teaching students about individuals who have positively impacted society and the world: (1) Ruby Bridges; (2) Jean-Michel Basquiat; (3) Naomi Osaka.
- Learning about character traits is a goal of the lesson, using IRA (intentional read-alouds with objectives stated at the beginning).
- Include adjectives that can describe character traits.
- Read-aloud activities help students identify actions and characters of people.
- Read-aloud books for the individuals are mentioned above.
- Engage students in discourse; use turn-and-talk activities for this. Turn and talk to your partner and discuss why you think a particular character trait is evident and what words in the story prove it (e.g., Basquiat was creative because he used different materials in his house to create things). Use this same approach for each of the three people being studied.

(U) Unlearning:

- *Student unlearning:* What about the laws were unfair and fair at the time? Discuss with students what segregation is and ask why they think everyone was not happy about Ruby Bridges attending school.

- Why did white families refuse to bring their children to school after Ruby started going to school? What are the misconceptions about white and Black people working together during that time?
- *Teacher unlearning:* How have myths or lack of information about integration misguided our understanding of a comprehensive history related to the truths of integrating and desegregating schools? What impact did integrating schools have for Black students, Black teachers, and Black neighborhoods?

(S) Stories:

- Students will create their own narrative using the idea of character traits for themselves.
- *Craftivity:* Self-portrait of themselves with character traits written, cut out, and glued around their self-portrait. This helps to introduce the idea of personal power and the fact that there are many aspects that make up who we are.
- *Final project:* Trace a silhouette of each student's entire body on butcher paper. Cut out the silhouette. Students do this to look at the world in a *bigger* way. This next step asks students to consider how they will make society better and how they will help others. Personal power = change. Students will label the parts of their silhouette with the goals they want to achieve by using personal power.

(H) Healing:

- Students will be offered an extra credit opportunity for service goals to use their personal power. Students can choose to help at home, at their church, in their neighborhood, and so on. Provide a menu of activity options for summative assessment. Create a photo album (labeling the photos to express what they did in partnerships with each other), a short poem, or a short song.

Close the lesson by allowing students to reflect and share out what they enjoyed about the lesson and activities.

MIDDLE/SECONDARY LESSON (SOCIAL STUDIES/HISTORY, GRADES 6–10)

Students Changing the Narrative: Freedom Summer and Student Non-Violent Coordinating Committee (SNCC)

Special thanks to social studies educator Katie Gehrt for collaborating.

Lesson Title: Students Changing the Narrative: Freedom Summer and Student Non-Violent Coordinating Committee (SNCC)

Courses: AP History/U.S. History/Social Studies
You can modify this lesson to include other groups such as AAPA (Asian American Political Alliance), ICSA (Intercollegiate Chinese for Social Action), PACE (Pilipino American Collegiate Endeavor), TWLF (Third World Liberation Front), or NASU (Native American Student Union)—all student groups active in the 1960s.

Lesson Description: This unit helps to illuminate Freedom Summer and SNCC (Student Non-Violent Coordinating Committee). This lesson offers students the opportunity to see the power of history and the pivotal role of young people in shifting social concerns and systemic inequities of the 1960s. The lesson asks us to consider what we can learn from the history of SNCC/civil rights and how we can apply that to today's concerns.

Essential Question: How do Freedom Summer and SNCC (Student Non-Violent Coordinating Committee) demonstrate the power of young people and how synergy among community members has the potential to effectively address societal problems?

Learning Objectives: Analyze and evaluate what Freedom Summer and SNCC entailed and how students can learn from these histories to enact change today. Examine and evaluate primary sources. Compare various perspectives about approaches related to educational equity, outreach, and the civil rights movement.

Materials/Instructional Resources:

- Presentation prepared by educator to teach about the historical context and foundational aspects of the lessons and activities.
- Freedom School background, curriculum, principles, and rationale (Seven Principles of Freedom Schools)
- Oral history: Charlie Cobb interview
- Primary source list and Mendy Samstein papers, 1963–1966
- SNCC Legacy Project

Instructional Strategies and Learning Tasks—Activating Prior Knowledge Phase:

Checking Your Bias:

- Dismantling myths about the history of education and access

Visual Introduction of Freedom Summer:

- Visual images of Freedom Summer
- Online "Report Cards" of current schools: students brainstorm list of current areas for improvement
- Video clips of Freedom Summer/SNCC

Core Components of the un/HUSH Framework:
(H) Histories:

1. Interview with Charlie Cobb
2. Mendy Samstein papers, 1963
3. Emphasis on structure and outreach
4. Excerpts from *The Freedom Schools* by Dr. Jon Hale

(U) Unlearning:

1. Reflection
2. Questions
    » What types of learning happened at Freedom Schools that couldn't happen at regular schools?
    » Hamer questioned whether the United States was "the land of the free and home of the brave." Do you think the United States lives up to this ideal today? Explain.

3. Activity
   - » Students will evaluate the structure and outreach of SNCC and events such as Freedom Summer, and how those events were collective endeavors that moved efforts toward change forward.

(S) Stories:

Quotes for unpacking:

- » "And you can always hear this long sob story: 'You know it takes time.' For three hundred years, we've given them time. And I've been tired so long, now I am sick and tired of being sick and tired, and we want a change."—*Fannie Lou Hamer*
- » "The people who run Mississippi today can only do so by force. They cannot allow a free election in Mississippi because if they did, they wouldn't run Mississippi."—*Al Lowenstein*
- » "We felt that we got what we called the Children of the Constitution, which were the white kids, to come in to bring more attention. People are going to be concerned about their children."—*Dave Dennis*
- » "These young people believed in democracy, and I think that they were volunteering because they were like true Americans. And what they were saying was I'm here to right a wrong that's being done to this country and democracy."—*Dave Dennis*
- » "If you're coming to Mississippi, you must know that you should be prepared to be beaten, to go to jail, and to be killed. And if you're not prepared for all three of those, we suggest that you go back home and do whatever you can to aid and assist the movement from there."—*Hollis Watkins*
- » "We were determined then they shall not have died in vain, so instead of intimidating us, it had the opposite effect on us."—*Ed King*
- » "All of this is on account of we want to register, to become first-class citizens. And if the Freedom Democratic Party is not seated now, I question America. Is this America, the land of the free and the home of the brave, where we have to sleep with our telephones off the hooks because our lives be threatened daily,

because we want to live as decent human beings, in America?"—*Fannie Lou Hamer*

(H) Healing:

1. Socratic seminar
2. Collaborative project
3. Comparison vs. contrast
4. Power of language activity
5. Collecting the stories of those before us—oral histories
6. Spoken history through timeline
7. School curriculum changes vs. Freedom Schools proposal

Lesson Activities
Initial Activity:

1. Look up report cards of neighboring districts and brainstorm a list of issues students and education are currently facing.
2. Examine the list of seven principles from the Freedom Schools (a few are listed below) and choose three that resonate with you and that you deem important. Notice how aspects of the Freedom School core beliefs align with un/HUSH, as they both utilize questions, community, and history to enhance learning—again ushering in the lessons of the past.
3. Next, create your own list of five principles that would effectively prepare students and address inequities in current-day education.
   » The creation of an honest and egalitarian relationship between teacher and student
   » The valuing and naming of the students' own experiences
   » The asking of open-ended questions
   » The presentation to students of an authentic and empowering view of themselves and their history
   » The vision of the arts as a transformative force

Final Project:

Step 1: Students will conduct and/or view a recorded and credible online oral history interview.
Step 2: Students can choose anyone who has been in education or formative in civil rights. Students should

strive to interview someone who was alive during the 1960s with a connection to education.

Step 3: Interviews can be conducted via Zoom or phone, or in person.

Step 4: If students choose to observe an oral history online, they will need to find a credible one (the Smithsonian and Library of Congress offer many resources).

Step 5: Students should refer to the questions in the "Student Guide to Oral Histories" in Appendix A to help begin planning their interview questions and strategy.

Step 6: Students will take notes during their interview and will analyze and discuss their answers in small groups.

Step 7: Students will present their findings, by focusing on three or four of the questions from the "Student Guide to Oral Histories" in Appendix A. Students can share out using a slide deck, visual aids, creative approaches (e.g., an object that represents the participant's story), a poster, or a short written synopsis.

Assessment: Assessment can be done using a rubric or in any manner most fitting for your classroom.

SECONDARY LESSON (HISTORY/MUSIC/ELA, GRADES 8–12)

Musical Storytelling: Perspectives, Solidarity, and Resistance During the 1960s

Special thanks to Taylor Masamitsu, educator and musician, for collaborating.

Lesson Title: Musical Storytelling: Perspectives, Solidarity, and Resistance During the 1960s

Suggested Courses: AP History/U.S. History/Music (History/Appreciation/Theory); grade levels 9–12 (could be modified for middle school)

Lesson Description: Social Studies/Music/ELA hybrid lesson that explores the inspirations for and reactions to civil protest music in the 1960s

Essential Question: How might the culture of protest music represent broader social, political, and/or racial relationships in the United States?

Learning Objectives: Students will analyze and evaluate specific songs (lyrics and music) from or about the 1960s to more comprehensively contextualize the civil rights era and contemporary issues of equity. Students will consider perspectives from a variety of musical sources, learn about public reactions to this music, and consider the foundational roles musicians have often played in shaping American culture (whether credited or not).

Materials/Instructional Resources:

- Evolution of American Protest Music—Vox (7 minutes)
- Rock and Roll Hall of Fame collection of interviews: https://library.rockhall.com/c.php?g=882116&p=6337961
- "Oxford Town" lyrics—Official Bob Dylan website
- "Blowin' in the Wind" lyrics—Official Bob Dylan website
- "Mississippi Goddam" lyrics—Nina Simone
    - » *Optional:* Essay with historical context from the Library of Congress
- Presentation prepared by the educator(s) to teach about the historical context and foundational aspects of the lessons and activities (e.g., oral tradition, the role of protest, etc.). Include a slide deck and handout with an overview and background information.
    - » In this presentation, we recommend highlighting at least two main points: accurate historical context *and* some of the racial inequities that materialized in the music industry during this time (see "Cadillac Car" resource).
- "Cadillac Car" lyrics two ways—*Dreamgirls* motion picture (2006)
- Print out lyrics of the songs used from the above options and find links for online viewing/listening. If desired, you might first examine the lyrics to select the best options for your particular students.

- Journal/discussion prompts (see questions below under Core Principles of the un/HUSH Framework).

Instructional Strategies and Learning Tasks: In this lesson, students will work collaboratively, individually, and as a class to discuss, analyze, and construct original multimedia pieces. These various works will allow students to (un)learn about diverse perspectives, acts of solidarity, and structural barriers associated with the American civil rights era in the 1960s. Ideally, students will exit this lesson with additional questions about whose perspectives remain unknown in conversations about American history, and have musical appreciation and resources for future investigation.

Core Principles of the un/HUSH Framework:
(H) Histories:

1. Evolution of American Protest Music—Vox (7 minutes)
2. In what ways has music historically connected groups as they worked toward collective change and equality?
3. What barriers have musicians/artists faced in using music/art to critique social structures?

(U) Unlearning for the Educator and/or Students:

1. How can we use music now to dismantle tropes, myths, or misinformation?
2. What can we learn about other cultures, communities, and people from music?
3. How have inequitable business practices in music (and beyond) come to exist? In what instances has cultural appropriation occurred in music and why? Can you think of and discuss music being co-opted from marginalized groups? What historical lessons might be connected to this?

(S) Stories:

1. How does music help facilitate stories, and why does music/art matter when we consider culturally responsive teaching?
2. What can you infer about the stories or messages found in the songs you listened to/the lyrics you analyzed/images consumed?

3. What are your impressions of the two versions of this song, and what do you notice about the two interpretations?

(H) Healing:

1. How has music historically helped facilitate healing, specifically in historically marginalized communities?
2. Has music today created understanding, healing, and connection/solidarity? If so, discuss further and offer specific examples.
3. What art (music, movies, TV, visual art, etc.) do you like? How does this artform/work impact you? How might it impact others like you? Unlike you?

Lesson Activities and Final Project(s):

Option 1: Create a playlist that includes songs celebrating connection, intersectionality, and diversity. To expand your own understanding and knowledge about groups different from your own, dedicate two songs each per group, and include a minimum of five different groups to research—this allows for research to occur across several different areas (time periods, cultural groups, etc.). For example, you might choose to research a Native American or Indigenous group, a Latinx group, an all-women's group, and so on. The only requirement is that the group did something related to protest, advocacy, or working as change agents.

Option 2: Create a playlist of 10 songs total that offers insights into the history of a group/culture/community whose history is not often known or shared. Your playlist should be chronological and thematically follow the history you discovered.

Table C.1 shares a few additional ideas for ways the project and activities could be utilized across disciplines.

The following are general questions to utilize for extended discussion or reflection:

1. What are your impressions of the two versions of this song?
2. What do you notice about the two interpretations?

Table C.1. Additional Activities

English Language Arts Course	History/Social Studies Course	Art Course	Music Course
Students can analyze song lyrics and discuss. Students can then create a poem showing they understand themes by using a patchwork of lyrics from the various songs (modified cento poem).	Students can create a timeline about broader historical events.	Students can draw coordinating images that help illustrate the meaning of the lyrics.	Students can use a small portion of one of the songs to analyze the chord progression or lyrics, or practice melodic dictation.
Students can collaborate by co-composing a synthesis about the songs' messages or rewrite one of the songs making it connected to today's concerns.	Students can create a timeline about the eras in which the songs emerged and discuss societal events that were salient at the time.	Students can engage in a visual thinking strategy that aligns with the historical aspects of the music being explored.	Students can consider their current environment and write a song (protest or otherwise) that represents the time/era.
Students can present about the songs' themes and inferences. Students can also compose original poems, lyrics, or other written works to synthesize their (un) learnings (collaboratively or individually).	Students can have a Socratic seminar discussing what they discovered in creating their timeline and exploring the era(s).	Students can co-create an art project that offers analysis and perspective about the lyrics and sentiments as they relate to current events.	Students can co-create an original song (music and/or lyrics) in the style of the analyzed song.

3. How might this scenario reflect real-life circumstances in professional and artistic spaces?
4. Is there a current song or video you can think of that both tells a story and advocates for social change, similar to protest songs? What can you analyze about the song and its similarities to protest songs?

5. What other groups came to mind during this project? What do you know about these histories?
6. What remains unknown? How might music or art help you learn more about it?

Assessment: Students will create a final playlist and choose one corresponding activity to demonstrate their learning. We encourage you to create a menu of options (see examples above for ideas). Consider everything from presentations to essays and visual displays. Offer students choice and the opportunity to be innovative.

SECONDARY LESSON AND MINI-UNIT (HISTORY/ELA, GRADES 8–12)

Unlikely Friendships and Intergroup Coalitions

Special thanks to Dr. Jon Hale and Chrissy Kim for collaborating.

Lesson Title: Unlikely Friendships and Intergroup Coalitions

Courses: English Language Arts/Dual Credit Literature/AP History/ U.S. History/Social Studies

This lesson can be modified to include Latinx, Native American, or other intergroup coalitions, such as the Young Lords Organization (YLO) or the Rainbow Coalition of the 1960s out of Chicago.

Mini-Unit Description: This unit helps to dismantle myths and bias by revealing the joy and power of unlikely intergroup coalitions and friendships. This unit celebrates those advancements and connections, and seeks to make their stories more visible, so that students can learn from the valuable lessons and strive toward the justice that these coalitions committed to.

Essential Question: How do unlikely coalitions or friendships deconstruct bias to create more cohesive classrooms?

Learning Objectives: Analyze and evaluate what it means to create coalitions and friendships that are connected through activism and equity. How did these unlikely duos work together? What myths or tropes do their friendships dismantle?

Materials/Instructional Resources:

- Presentation prepared by the educator to teach about the historical context and foundational aspects of the lessons and activities
- Resource list
- Cento/elegy poetry list
- Lesson presentation slide deck

Instructional Strategies and Learning Tasks—Activating Prior Knowledge Phase:

Checking Your Bias:

- Dismantling myths about the model minority

Visual Introduction of Coalitions:

- Highlighting parallels between the depiction of Asian people and Black Americans throughout U.S. history
- Modern murals created together by AAPI and Black artists/activists

Introduction of Primary Sources:

- What are they?
- How do we use them?
- Defining credible resources and research

Core Components of the un/HUSH Framework:
(H) Histories:

1. Treasure hunt for primary sources
2. Divide students into small groups. Each group will have an envelope containing artifacts and sources relating to Yuri Kochiyama, Grace Lee Boggs, or Cathy Park Hong. Students will discuss sources and histories.

3. Emphasis on coalition and collaboration efforts
4. Students will examine and discuss the collaboration of people such as Grace Lee Boggs and James Boggs, Malcolm X and Yuri Kochiyama, and others to examine how different groups can work together.

(U) Unlearning:

1. Reflection
2. Questions
   - What might you need to know more about to teach these histories to others?
   - How might your positionality inform any bias related to the content?
   - Where can you find sources that offer accurate information?

(S) Stories: Students will complete a jigsaw and flash biographies to examine the different elements of the lesson: Malcolm X's life, Yuri Kochiyama's life, context and events of the 1960s, and perhaps other unlikely friendships or partnerships of the 1960s. Students will work in groups and then share out their findings and flash biographies, centering their voices and offering self-efficacy and autonomy in learning.

(H) Healing:

1. Socratic seminar
2. Collaborative project
3. Presentation based on flash memoirs and sources to share what they learned about the person and story they researched
4. Students will write elegy or cento poems to celebrate and honor the lives of the unlikely coalitions and friendships they explored. Students can of course draw conclusions related to their own lives and then share out their poems.

Lesson Activities—Initial Activity:

1. Students will explore the stories and lives of others (both historic and current). In the same groups, students will craft a flash biography/memoir of the person they explored (100–300 words). This activity provides an opportunity for students to practice planning and editing a narrative, as well as utilizing literacy devices.

2. Create presentation to share out information.
3. Elegy or cento poems

Assessment: Students will work in pairs to answer the following essay prompt:

> Imagine how two individuals we have learned about in class from the AAPI and Black communities, respectively, would work together to address a modern social issue (e.g., affirmative action, immigration, voting rights, etc.). To support your ideas, use a minimum of three sources (artifacts, primary sources, secondary sources, poems).

This lesson shows the flexibility and adaptability of the framework.

POSTSECONDARY LESSON PLAN

Moral Foundations and Logical Fallacies

Special thanks to Jordan Stempleman, professor and poet, for collaborating.

Lesson Title: Moral Foundations and Logical Fallacies

Lesson Description: This lesson engages undergraduates enrolled in a 1st-year writing seminar in a discussion about morality and what frames our understanding of the subject. This lesson helps students self-assess and better understand logical fallacies and positionality.

Essential Question: How do the stories we tell ourselves shape our understanding of ourselves and others, and oftentimes create forms of bias and fallacies that prevent rational engagement with others and our thinking.

Learning Objectives: Analyze and evaluate what it means to create coalitions and friendships that are connected through activism and equity. How did these unlikely individuals or groups work together? What myths or tropes do their friendships dismantle?

Materials/Instructional Resources:

- Joan Didion's essay "On Morality"
- Comparison of Kant's and Hegel's arguments about the rational mind (it is optional to use these as supplemental texts and to include this as part of the lesson)
- TED Talk: "The Moral Matrix" by Jonathan Haidt
- Lecture related to foundational ideas and examples from Jonathan Haidt's book *The Righteous Mind*
- Logical fallacies list (from Annenberg Foundation's example and lesson about fallacies) and explanation with Aristotle's rhetorical triangle
- Examples of primary sources and two or three historical individuals who grappled with and discussed morality
- Supplemental text: "Dear Joshua" essay by Margaret Alvarado (this essay examines loss and healing)

Instructional Strategies and Learning Tasks: This lesson would ideally occur in two 3-hour class sessions.

Step 1: Students will initially read Joan Didion's essay "On Morality" before the lesson begins; this can be assigned as prereading before class. A close read of the essay will be led by the professor, and a discussion and analysis will follow. The professor/instructor will overview: The author, Didion, says we use the term "morality" in an unwieldy way, and that as we get outside of any given cultural context, the term morality starts to change. Didion's argument is that morality is dependent on the cultural context that you are in. Students will be asked to consider Didion's argument.

Step 2: Next, students will view a TED Talk called "The Moral Matrix" by Jonathan Haidt, social psychologist, where he outlines the five fundamental pillars of morality. After students learn about the five foundational categories that guide our moral thinking and sensibility (harm/care, fairness/reciprocity, in-group loyalty, authority/respect, purity/sanctity), students will again engage in a discussion and analysis of the information. What students will likely discover in this TED Talk is that we all care about these categories to some degree, but depending on where and how we were raised (our positionality), we value a number of these categories over others. The goal of the TED Talk is to discover how we can come together, despite our differences. Haidt queried people and discovered that these categories align themselves with our social and political views. Students will then take the Moral Foundations Questionnaire to discover where they fall in regard to these values. What you will likely see is how diverse the classroom population is. Next, the class will discuss the results and their experiences taking the questionnaire.

Step 3: Lastly, the professor will move students into small groups (three or four groups), where students will examine the historical moral questioning of others and then move toward discussing their own questioning. This will expose students to histories and illustrate the various ways humans grapple with morality (if time is short, this portion of the lesson can be assigned as prereading). Students can then share their stories about why they scored high or low in their categories. They will be asked to share one story where they share their histories about why their score was what it was (e.g., perhaps a coach inspired the student, and that gave the student a strong foundation of respect). This experience helps students discover and analyze what shaped them and helps them to understand their histories and the histories of others. The unlearning component of the framework will occur as the class moves into later discussions of logical fallacies and the reflection process of being self-reflective of our own views and beliefs. The TED Talk, group discussions, and activities will all contribute to the unlearning component through self-reflection, which the professor will also take part in. The professor can choose to show students how they scored on the test previously from years ago and today—illustrating how self-reflection spurs growth.

Healing is examined in this lesson using self-assessment and discussion. The instructor can choose to assign extended reading such as "Dear Joshua" by Mary Margaret Alvarado. Healing can be discussed by exploring what shapes our moral foundations and the resistance we have to others' beliefs and traditions. The lesson will be used to build forthcoming assignments, close readings of texts, and writing.

30-Day Challenge Topics for Extended Learning

In Figure D.1 you will find key words and topics that I believe are helpful in shaping our knowledge of both history and other cultures. This, of course, is not an exhaustive list, but a starting place. I invite you to take 30 days to research each one and learn more. This task is intended for you (the educator) but could be shared with your students or incorporated into a learning activity.

Figure D.1. Learning Challenge

30 DAY LEARNING CHALLENGE

Illuminating Inclusive Histories

DAY 1	DAY 2	DAY 3	DAY 4	DAY 5
Black Wall Street	Native American Boarding Schools	Rough Rock Demonstration SchooL	Internment Camps and "My Plea" by Mary M.	The Chinese Exclusion Act
DAY 6	**DAY 7**	**DAY 8**	**DAY 9**	**DAY 10**
Lau v. Nichols	Mamie Tape Case	Model Minority Myth	Plessy v. Ferguson and Brown v. Board	Stonewall Uprising
DAY 11	**DAY 12**	**DAY 13**	**DAY 14**	**DAY 15**
Student Non-Violent Coordinating Committee (SNCC)	The Friendship of Malcolm X and Yuri Kochiyama	Angel Island Poetry	People v. Hall (1854)	The Bellingham Riots of 1907
DAY 16	**DAY 17**	**DAY 18**	**DAY 19**	**DAY 20**
Filipino Farmers Grape Strike	Indian Citizenship Act	The Combahee River Collective	The Chitlin Circuit	Igbo Landing
DAY 21	**DAY 22**	**DAY 23**	**DAY 24**	**DAY 25**
Compensated Emancipation Act of 1862	Mendez v. Westminster or The Chicano Blowouts	Redlining and Blockbusting	Carter G. Woodson	The Zoot Suit Riots
DAY 26	**DAY 27**	**DAY 28**	**DAY 29**	**DAY 30**
The Black Codes	Bob Moses, Charlie Cobb, Freedom Summer	Mildred Loving, Fannie Lou Hamer, Ida B. Wells	Gordon Parks	Judith Heumann, Johnnie Lacy, Leroy Moore

Additional Educator Reflection Prompts

Writing is powerful, and words help us evaluate and assess our thoughts and beliefs. Listed below are some additional prompts for reflection. These questions would also make good discussion starters or free writing prompts for students.

- What creates your perspective, and from what lens do you view the world? Consider your positionality.
- What are the greatest challenges you need to overcome regarding your own learning?
- What areas of instruction/social–emotional learning/ cultural competency/curriculum design/and so forth do you feel most comfortable with and why? Where would you like more information or guidance?
- What do you think would best support your work as an educator?
- If you could expand your own knowledge in two areas, what would they be and why?
- How can curriculum be used as a tool to help develop cultural competency and equity?
- What is one new instructional strategy you are willing to try this semester/year?
- If you could change one thing about your classroom, what would it be and why?
- What works well in your classroom? Make a list.
- What is one lesson or procedure you need to let go of, and why?
- bell hooks said, "Rarely, if ever, are any of us healed in isolation. Healing is an act of communion." How can you apply this sentiment to your teaching?

List of Poetic Forms

There are several poetic forms that fit easily into the classroom and make excellent ways for students to demonstrate their learning. In no specific order, I have listed a few that I have used often below, but there are of course many more poetic forms to explore and consider.

- **Cento Poem:** A cento poem is a "patchwork poem" consisting of 100 lines borrowed from other poems/poets. This form allows students to explore a theme and styles without the pressure of producing their own words and lines. How they arrange the lines is what makes a cento impactful. An important aspect of the cento is teaching students to properly credit each poet for lines they quote and borrow. This activity exposes students to a variety of poets, forms, themes, and so forth. This has been one of my favorite forms to use with students, as I have coupled it with research and used it to teach theme.
- **Epistle Poem:** Epistle poems are essentially letters written in verse. An example of how you might use this would be to ask students to write a letter modeled after Langston Hughes's poem "Theme for English B." This is a great activity to use at the beginning of the year to help you learn more about your students, and it helps students understand voice and tone.
- **Ode Poem:** Ode poems are short poems that celebrate or praise a person, idea, or event. This is a poetic form that works well with any grade level and works with almost any teaching unit. An example of an ode poem is "Ode to Ethiopia" by Paul Laurence Dunbar.
- **Erasure Poem/Blackout Poem:** Erasure poems (also known as blackout poems) are a form of found poetry that allows students to "erase" or strike out words from an existing

piece of text to craft a poem. This can be done using old newspapers, magazines, or online sites that offer erasure poem templates.

- **Spoken Word Poetry:** Spoken word poetry is a great way to allow students the freedom to explore words and free verse poetry. Spoken word allows students to orally perform their poetry and is a great form to build confidence and give students practice in presenting and speaking in front of an audience.
- **Upside-Down Poem:** Upside-down poems take a previously written poem and rearrange the lines and stanzas to create a new poem.
- **Object Poem:** Object poems are a form of poetry that uses objects as the subject matter. This might include everyday objects or objects with important meaning. An example of an object poem is "The Red Wheelbarrow" by William Carlos Williams. This form works well with all ages and is an easily adaptable for most subjects.
- **Ekphrastic Poem:** Ekphrasis poetry is written about works of art or in response to a visual work (e.g., the cover of a news article, a historical image, an artwork, etc.). This is a great way to combine art and poetry by showing students a visual image and asking them to craft a poem based on that image. This helps with synthesis, reading an image, and understanding the importance of symbolism, setting, and so forth.
- **Pictographic Poem or Photopoetry:** Pictographic poems or photopoetry are poems crafted so that the words of the poem form a picture. This is a form that appeals to many students, as it combines text with the visual.
- **Catalog Poem:** Catalog poems are poems that involve a list, and consist of the enumeration of people, feelings, ideas, and so forth. This form is a great way to teach comparisons and similarities. An example of a catalog poem is "Catalog of Unabashed Gratitude" by Ross Gay.
- **Free Verse Poetry:** Free verse poetry is an open form with nonrhyming, nonmetrical lines of poetry that allows students to explore the freedom of choice in what they write and how they construct the poem. Free verse poems are some of my favorites, and there are so many examples of this form. One example that comes to mind is "Still I Rise" by Maya Angelou.

- **Six-Word Memoir:** Six-word memoirs are inspired by author Ernest Hemingway, and they are short poems made up of six words only. This poem is a great way for students to begin or end an activity, as it asks them to consider the whole, sum it up, and then write with brevity. You can see many examples at https://www.sixwordmemoirs.com.
- **Golden Shovel Poem:** The golden shovel is a poetic form in which you take a line (or several lines) from a poem. Next, you use each word in the line(s) as an end word of a line in your new poem. An example of a golden shovel is "The Golden Shovel" by Terrance Hayes, using Gwendolyn Brooks's poem "We Real Cool" as the inspiration poem. This poem and most others mentioned above can be found at https://www.poetryfoundation.org.

Index

About the Author

Marlee S. Bunch is an interdisciplinary educator with well over a decade of teaching experience. She holds a doctoral degree from the University of Illinois in Education Policy, Organization and Leadership (with a concentration in diversity/equity/inclusion). She also holds a Master's in Education and a Master's of Science in Gifted Education. She holds a teaching certificate with endorsements in both English Language Arts and Social Studies, a Gifted Education Certification, an English Language Learner (ELL/ESL) Certification, and a Diversity and Equity Certificate.

Dr. Bunch's experiences teaching at the secondary and postsecondary level have allowed her to write curriculum, mentor teachers, create workshops, and most importantly, support students. She has taught English Literature, Creative Writing, Adult Education, and Composition.

Her research, teaching, and scholarship seek to disrupt inequities and illuminate the power of storytelling and history. Her research examines Black female educators in Mississippi between 1954 and 1971 and the impact history and desegregation had on their lives and current day education. Dr. Bunch is a mentor for students and uses writing and history to encourage dialogue and self-reflection. She has forthcoming publications with the University of Illinois Press and a coauthored book with Routledge. She is a National Academy of Education Spencer Fellowship semi-finalist. For additional information and resources, or to contact Dr. Bunch, please visit https://www.marleebunch.com.

The Magnitude of Us

By Will Adams (former student)

(Written to celebrate *The Magnitude of Us* book and our time spent in the classroom together.)

We sat in circles,
Strangers bound by schedules and seats,
Passing looks like fleeting moments,
Not knowing how close we'd become.
A place of public education turned parish for private pondering
Words spilled out like secrets long held in our throats—
Each voice cracked open,
Each heart peeled bare like pages we forgot to read.

This room, four walls, but it felt bigger—
Like the world shrank down and lived in here
Between desks and shared breaths,
Between thoughts left hanging and answers found
Not in textbooks, but in the eyes of the ones
We never thought we'd call friends.

In the silence after someone's truth,
We learned to listen, not to respond, but to feel.
To feel what it means to be human,
To carry the weight of someone else's story
Like it was our own,
And for a moment,
We were no longer a room full of individuals—
We were us.

The magnitude of us was in the vulnerability,
In the spaces between the words
Where we met each other's wounds with understanding
And sewed stitches with shared respect.

We came in with masks,
Tied tight with strings of pride and pretense,
Thinking we knew ourselves,
But these Socratic circles—

We're more like mirrors than glass.
Each question pulled at the seams of our silence,
Until we unraveled, thread by thread,
And there, in that unraveling, we were free.

It wasn't just about the syllabus,
It was about the way we showed up, raw and real,
Trading small talk for big truths.
We were more than the roles we played
We shattered those molds when we spoke.
Young girls growing into women and boys to men
A chorus of voices that shouldn't have harmonized,
But somehow, in that space, we did.

That shift, that spark, when someone said something
That hit home,
And you realized we weren't so different after all.
We were all searching,
Trying to figure out where we fit
In this chaotic, unplanned masterpiece of life.

We found pieces of ourselves
In the stories others were brave enough to share.
And with each revelation,
The walls we built outside this room crumbled,
Brick by brick, until what was left
Was something solid.
A foundation of respect,
Of trust.

When the final bell rang,
And when the desks were pushed back into rows
We carried it with us.
Not just the lessons from books,
But the lessons from each other.
The magnitude of us wasn't something confined to that
classroom—
It stretches far beyond those walls,
Echoing in the choices we make,
In the way we see and hear the world now.

We walked out different,
Not because we had all the answers,
But because we learned to ask the right questions.
We understood that empathy isn't a quiet nod,
It's a force,
That vulnerability isn't weakness,
It's the gravity that holds us together.

I still think about it sometimes—
How those moments shaped us,
How they taught us to step outside ourselves,
To look beyond what's on the surface
And see the person standing next to us
Not just as a peer,
But as a story unfolding.

Now we're scattered,
Each of us on different paths,
But there's a thread that still binds us,
A thread woven in those moments,
In those shared truths and silent understandings.

The magnitude of us isn't just in numbers,
It's in the weight of the words we shared,
In the gravity of connection we formed.
The magnitude of us
Isn't measured by time spent together,
But by the space we created for one another—
A space that still lives within us,
Expanding,
Ever-growing,
An unmeasurable force.
Because the magnitude of us
Was never about how many we were,
But about how deeply we connected.

An audio recording of this poem is available at the Teachers College Press website at https://teachers-college-press.myshopify.com/products/the-magnitude-of-us_9780807769881. The materials appear at the bottom of the web page.

NOTES

NOTES

NOTES